Unlocking
Language

From Syntax to Semantics:
A Comprehensive Exploration

Liam Connors

TABLE OF CONTENTS

Introduction

Welcome to "Unlocking Language: From Syntax to Semantics - A Comprehensive Exploration." Language is a cornerstone of human communication, a complex tapestry woven with the threads of syntax and semantics. This e-book embarks on a transformative journey into the intricacies of language structure and meaning, aiming to demystify the often-overlooked nuances that shape our everyday communication.

We examine syntax fundamentals in the first few chapters, dissecting the components of sentences and examining the various linguistic patterns. From the fundamental roles of nouns and verbs to the subtle intricacies of syntax in different linguistic families, readers will gain a solid understanding of how language is structured.

The exploration continues into semantics, where we dissect the layers of meaning embedded in words and expressions. Semantic fields, relations, and the exciting interaction between language and culture are all examined in this section. Semantic analysis's practical uses shed more light on how words influence our relationships and perceptions.

Moving beyond syntax and semantics, we delve into pragmatics, examining how context, culture, and communicative intent influence language use. The exciting relationships between language, cognition, and embodied cognition are then brought to light by cognitive linguistics.

As we journey through the pages of this e-book, we also explore the evolutionary roots of language, unraveling theories on its origin and tracing its development in the human species. The concluding chapters look ahead, examining cutting-edge effects in linguistics, such as the nexus between linguistics and artificial intelligence and breakthroughs in computers.

"Unlocking Language" is an invitation to understand the instrument's depth and richness that defines our existence, links us to others, and molds our thinking, not just an exploration. Whether you're a language enthusiast, a student, or someone seeking a deeper understanding of the essence of communication, this comprehensive guide is your key to unlocking the captivating world of language.

Chapter I

Foundations of Syntax

Definition and Scope of Syntax

Language, the cornerstone of human communication, is a remarkably intricate system, and at its core lies the essential framework of syntax. The set of guidelines that define how words are structured to create sense in sentences is known as syntax or grammar in some other languages. We'll look at the definition and usage of syntax in this investigation, revealing the connections that hold words together to create clear and expressive speech.

The study of sentence construction is syntax at its most basic level. It creates the rules defining the proper structure of words and sentences in a given language to convey meaning. Grammar serves as a guide for creating grammatically and semantically sound phrases, enabling people to share their ideas and thoughts precisely.

The primary objective of syntax is to understand the relationships between words and how these relationships add to a sentence's overall meaning. It investigates how comments function within a sentence—identifying subjects, verbs, objects, and other grammatical elements. By examining the syntactic structure, linguists can discern a sentence's intended meaning and nuances.

Syntax has more uses than just building sentences. It comprises the hierarchical arrangement of linguistic components, highlighting the relationships between various sentence components. We break down sentences, clauses, and phrase structures to expose the underlying concepts that guide their construction. Syntax also examines word categories—such as nouns, verbs, adjectives, and adverbs—to understand how word categories convey specific meanings.

One of the critical aspects of syntax is understanding the differences in sentence structure across languages. While the basic syntactic principles may be universal, each language exhibits unique syntactic characteristics and rules. As a result, syntax serves as a tool for comparative linguistics, allowing researchers to examine the variety of linguistic structures and identify the distinctive ways other languages express meaning.

Sentences are more than just collections of words when it comes to syntax; they are well-planned sequences with rules governing word agreement, tense, and order. The study of syntax sheds light on these rules, offering insights into how languages encode information and convey relationships between entities. It provides a framework for understanding the grammatical principles speakers intrinsically follow while constructing sentences, enhancing the coherence and comprehensibility of communication.

Moreover, syntax is not static; it evolves over time, reflecting changes in language use and societal norms. Linguists study historical syntax to trace the evolution of sentence structures, uncovering shifts in grammatical rules and syntactic patterns across different periods. This historical perspective enhances our understanding of how languages develop and adapt, offering a lens through which we can observe the dynamic nature of linguistic systems.

Additionally, syntax is essential to a child's growth in language acquisition. As individuals learn a language, they internalize its syntactic structures, gradually grasping the rules that govern sentence formation. Syntax, therefore, serves as a cognitive tool that aids in language development, influencing how individuals comprehend and produce language from the earliest stages of learning.

In conclusion, syntax is the intricate framework that underlies language structure, providing the guidelines and precepts that control word combinations to produce meaningful communication. Its scope extends beyond the construction of sentences, encompassing the hierarchical organization of linguistic elements and the comparative analysis of syntactic structures across languages. Syntax is a dynamic field, offering insights into the evolution of language over time and playing a pivotal role in language acquisition. We develop a greater understanding of the intricacy and beauty inherent in how we organize and communicate our ideas through language as we go through the complexities of syntax.

Basic Sentence Structures

In the vast tapestry of human communication, sentences serve as the fundamental building blocks, weaving together words to convey meaning. Understanding the intricacies of basic sentence structures is essential for anyone seeking mastery of a language. This exploration will delve into the various components and types of basic sentence structures, examining how syntax shapes the foundation of coherent expression.

A phrase is a piece of text that fully describes an idea. It typically consists of a subject, a verb, and an object, forming the basic structure known as a "subject-verb-object" (SVO) construction. This structure is a common feature across many languages and provides a clear and concise way to convey information. For example, in the sentence "The cat (subject) chased (verb) the mouse (object)," each component plays a distinct role in conveying the action and the entities involved.

Nevertheless, only some phrases follow the SVO form. Languages exhibit remarkable diversity in sentence constructions, and variations in word order contribute to the richness of linguistic expression. For example, the "subject-object-verb" (SOV) structure is typical in languages like Turkish and Japanese. In a sentence like "I (subject) sushi (object) eat (verb)" in Japanese, the subject comes first, followed by the object and the verb. Examining these variants demonstrates how linguistic systems are adaptive and flexible.

Languages have "subject-verb" (SV) and "subject-object" (SO) constructions in addition to the fundamental SVO and SOV structures. In these simplified forms, sentences retain grammatical completeness with only the subject and verb or subject and object, respectively. For example, in the SV structure, "The sun (subject) rises (verb)" expresses a complete thought without the inclusion of a direct object.

Another essential aspect of basic sentence structures involves the identification of sentence types. Declarative sentences make statements or express opinions, interrogative sentences pose questions, imperative sentences give commands, and exclamatory sentences convey strong emotions. Every kind performs a different communicative role, demonstrating how the placement of words inside a sentence can express the speaker's intention and emotional tone in addition to facts.

As we navigate the landscape of basic sentence structures, we encounter the concept of clauses—groups of words containing a subject and a verb that may function independently as complete sentences or as components within more significant penalties. Independent sentences are self-contained, whereas dependent phrases rely on an independent clause for completeness. Combining independent and dependent clauses allows for the creation of complex sentences, enriching the expressive capacity of language.

Compound and complex sentences have more complex sentence structures. There are two or more independent clauses in a compound sentence, joined by coordinating conjunctions like "and," "but," or "or." To illustrate related notions, consider the statement, "She loves reading, and he enjoys writing," which connects two independent clauses. Conversely, complex sentences incorporate both independent and dependent clauses. In the ruling "Although it was raining, they decided to go for a walk," the independent clause "they decided to go for a walk" is accompanied by the dependent clause "Although it was raining."

Understanding basic sentence structures also requires an exploration of modifiers—words or phrases that provide additional information about other elements in a sentence. Adjectives modify nouns, adverbs modify verbs, and prepositional phrases change various features by indicating relationships in time, space, or manner. Including modifiers enhances language richness and specificity, allowing speakers and writers to paint vivid pictures with their words.

Furthermore, sentence patterns can change as a result of a variety of syntactic processes. Passive voice, for example, allows for a shift in emphasis by altering the traditional subject-verb-object order. In the active voice sentence, "The chef (subject) cooked (verb) a delicious meal (object)," the passive voice version becomes "A delicious meal (subject) was cooked (verb) by the chef," emphasizing the meal rather than the chef.

An exploration of basic sentence structures is complete with addressing the role of punctuation in clarifying meaning and facilitating comprehension. Commas, periods, question marks, and exclamation points serve as signposts, guiding readers through the flow of ideas and indicating pauses, stops, questions, or emphatic statements. Proficiency in punctuation enhances communication effectiveness by guaranteeing accurate transmission of the intended idea.

To summarize, fundamental sentence patterns are the cornerstone of successful communication because they offer the necessary structure for expressing concepts, ideas, and feelings. The study of syntax sheds light on sentence construction, covering everything from the basic SVO form to the differences in word order throughout languages. Understanding sentence types, clauses, and syntactic processes enriches language proficiency, enabling individuals to navigate the dynamic landscape of linguistic expression. As we unravel the intricacies of basic sentence structures, we gain a deeper appreciation for the artistry of language and the tools to communicate with clarity and precision.

Parts of Speech

In the grand orchestration of language, the parts of speech are the instrumental players, each with its unique role and contribution to the melody of communication. These linguistic elements—nouns, verbs, adjectives, and conjunctions—form the fundamental building blocks that enable us to communicate thoughts clearly and nuancedly. We will examine the meanings, purposes, and interactions of the various components of speech in the language symphony as we delve into their complexities.

The foundational words of the language represent the names of people, places, things, or concepts. They serve as the focal points of sentences, giving them the specificity required for clear communication. Whether the tangible "mountain" standing majestically on the horizon or the intangible "freedom" many seek, nouns encapsulate what we wish to convey. Moreover, nouns can be further classified into common nouns, such as "dog" or "city," and proper nouns, such as "Rover" or "Paris," adding layers of specificity to our linguistic repertoire.

The dynamic agents of expression propel sentences forward with action or state of being. From the swift "run" of an athlete to the contemplative "think" of a philosopher, verbs breathe life into our communications. The various tenses of verbs—past, present, and future—allow us to navigate the temporal landscape of language, providing context and precision. Understanding the nuances of verb usage is paramount, as it determines the tone, mood, and timing of our expressions.

The description artists imbue nouns with qualities, creating striking mental pictures for our readers. Whether it's the "sparkling" ocean or the "mysterious" stranger, adjectives amplify the impact of nouns, adding color and texture to our narratives. Their placement within a sentence is strategic, influencing the overall tone and emphasis. Adjectives play a crucial role in evoking sensory experiences and shaping the emotional resonance of language.

The versatile companions of verbs, adjectives, and other adverbs contribute nuance by providing information about how, when, where, or to what degree an action or condition occurs. The adverb "quickly" modifies the verb "run," transforming a simple step into a sprint. Adverbs, subtly or emphatically, guide the reader or listener through the narrative, offering additional layers of detail and context.

The linguistic chameleons stand in for nouns, reducing redundancy and promoting fluidity in communication. The use of pronouns improves efficiency and clarity. Examples of these are the demonstrative pronouns "this" and "those," which point to specific elements, and the personal pronouns "he," "she," or "they," which simplify references to individuals. The selection of pronouns affects the language's formality and tone, promoting a feeling of comfort or expertise.

The linguistic network's connectors, which indicate location, direction, time, or manner, help form linkages between a phrase's many parts. Whether it's the cat "on" the roof or the meeting scheduled "for" tomorrow, prepositions create spatial and temporal frameworks that anchor language in the real world.

The coordinators and subordinators orchestrate the flow of ideas by connecting words, phrases, or clauses. Coherent conjunctions such as "and," "but," and "or" allow you to secure items that are equally important while maintaining cohesion and fluidity. Conjunctions that subordinate, including "although," "because," and "while," establish dependent clauses and give sentence structures more nuance and complexity.

Language is punctuated with exclamations, greetings, or expressions of surprise to reflect emotional outbursts. Interjections, such as the gregarious "Wow!" or the casual "Hey," lend an element of spontaneity and genuineness to our communication. While often standing alone or set off by punctuation, interjections contribute to spoken and written language's dynamic and interactive nature.

As we navigate the rich tapestry of the parts of speech, it becomes evident that their roles are not isolated; they collaborate in intricate ways to construct meaning and convey nuances. The selection and arrangement of words within a sentence involve a dance among these linguistic components, each playing its part in creating harmonious and effective communication.

Furthermore, knowing the components of speech encompasses more than just grammar; it also involves style and rhetoric. A proficient writer or orator intentionally utilizes the many features of speech to compose phrases that capture, convince, or arouse feelings. Consider the deliberate use of vivid adjectives in a poem to paint a sensory landscape or the strategic deployment of powerful verbs in a persuasive essay to convey conviction and authority. Mastery of the parts of speech provides the tools for linguistic artistry.

The interplay of parts of speech is also a crucial aspect of language acquisition. As individuals learn a new language, grasping the functions and nuances of nouns, verbs, and other components is essential for effective communication. Teachers and students work through the subtleties of sentence construction, gradually internalizing the standards and conventions that regulate the use of every part of speech.

To sum up, the components of speech constitute the fundamental building blocks of language, skillfully arranging the communication symphony. Prepositions, conjunctions, interjections, verbs, adjectives, adverbs, pronouns, and contribute a unique melody to the linguistic composition. Understanding the functions and relationships between these grammatical components opens new possibilities for expressive and sophisticated communication and improving grammar competency. As we explore the depths of language, we unravel the intricacies of these linguistic components, appreciating the symphonic beauty they bring to our conversations, stories, and expressions.

Syntax in Different Languages

Language, the vibrant tapestry of human expression, weaves a myriad of sounds, words, and grammatical structures together. At the heart of linguistic diversity lies syntax—the arrangement of words to form meaningful sentences. Yet, as we explore syntax across different languages, we encounter a fascinating array of patterns, rules, and variations that shape the structure of communication. This exploration invites us to appreciate the richness of linguistic diversity while highlighting how syntax serves as a unique cultural and cognitive fingerprint for each language.

One striking aspect of syntax is the variation in word order, a feature that distinguishes the sentence structures of different languages. The English language, for instance, predominantly follows a Subject-Verb-Object (SVO) word order, as seen in the sentence, "The cat (subject) chased (verb) the mouse (object)." Contrastingly, languages like Japanese and Turkish often employ a Subject-Object-Verb (SOV) word order, as demonstrated in the Japanese sentence "Watashi (I, subject) sushi (sushi, object) tabemasu (eat, verb)." This structural variation extends beyond SVO and SOV, encompassing Subject-Verb (SV) and Subject-Object (SO) languages, illustrating the dynamic ways languages construct meaning through the organization of words.

Furthermore, case marks add another level of complexity to syntax since different languages use different methods to show the grammatical links between words. Cases alter nouns and pronouns to indicate their grammatical function in a phrase in languages such as Latin and Russian. The absence of case markings in languages like English or Chinese necessitates reliance on word order and context to convey grammatical relationships.

The syntax's flexibility is evident in verb conjugation, where verbs change forms to indicate various grammatical features such as tense, aspect, mood, and person. Romance languages like Spanish and French are known for their rich verb conjugation systems, where each verb form reflects specific grammatical information. Conversely, verb conjugation is comparatively more straightforward in English, relying more on auxiliary verbs and word order to convey temporal nuances.

Syntax also plays a pivotal role in expressing politeness and formality in language. The choice of verb forms and sentence structures in languages such as Korean and Japanese is closely related to social hierarchies and speaker relationships. Varying levels of politeness are encoded in the syntax, reflecting cultural values of respect and social harmony. Contrastingly, languages such as English and Dutch rely more on lexical choices and explicit markers to convey politeness.

Furthermore, the treatment of gender in syntax is a linguistic feature that varies significantly across languages. While languages like Spanish and French assign grammatical gender to nouns, requiring agreement in articles and adjectives, languages like English have a more straightforward approach. The diversity of ways that languages arrange and categorize material is emphasized by the fact that pronouns are commonly employed to express gender in English, a language lacking grammatical gender.

Syntax is deeply entwined with cultural nuances, influencing how speakers convey meaning and express social norms. In Navajo, a Native American language, the verb structure reflects the speaker's direct sensory experience, incorporating information about touch, sight, and motion. This is an example of how cultural perspectives can be encoded by syntax, giving insight into the worldview of a group. Honorifics are used in Korean grammar to indicate respect and reflect the culture's emphasis on hierarchical relationships.

The cognitive aspects of syntax provide an intriguing window into the human mind's potential for language, independent of cultural influences. Psycholinguistic research indicates that speakers of different languages can have different syntax processing strategies, which reflect the linguistic patterns inherent in their home tongues. The cognitive demands of processing complex sentence structures, such as those found in German or Finnish, highlight the remarkable adaptability of the human brain in navigating diverse syntactic landscapes.

The syntax of sign languages, a unique linguistic modality, further underscores the universality of syntactic principles across languages. For instance, American Sign Language (ASL) exhibits syntactic structures similar to those found in spoken languages. Grammar links are conveyed through the arrangement of signals, the usage of facial expressions, and body language, demonstrating the flexibility of syntax in supporting communication in various linguistic contexts.

Furthermore, how historical and geographic contexts affect syntax sheds light on the dynamic evolution of language. As a result of contact between several linguistic communities, creole languages frequently have simpler syntax than their parent languages. African American English's syntax, influenced by the African diaspora's historical background, exhibits distinctive syntactic characteristics that have developed over time, illuminating the complex relationship between language structure, history, and culture.

As we traverse the diverse syntactic landscapes of different languages, it becomes clear that syntax is not a monolithic entity but a dynamic and adaptive system shaped by linguistic, cultural, and cognitive factors. Syntax bridges the abstract realm of meaning and the tangible expressions of language, embodying the creativity and diversity inherent in human communication.

In conclusion, the exploration of syntax across different languages unveils a rich mosaic of structures, rules, and variations that contribute to the uniqueness of each linguistic system. From word order and case markings to verb conjugation and cultural influences, syntax reflects the intricate interplay of cognitive, cultural, and historical factors. Embracing the diversity of syntactic patterns enhances our understanding of language as a dynamic and evolving phenomenon, showcasing the boundless creativity encoded in the structures that underpin human communication.

Chapter II

Syntax in Practice

Syntax and Sentence Construction

In linguistics, Syntax stands as the architectural blueprint, guiding the construction of sentences that convey meaning, intent, and nuance. The complex dance of words inside the syntactic framework creates the background language used to express itself in all forms. This investigation explores the mutually beneficial link between sentence structure and Syntax, revealing the rules guiding how we arrange words to produce meaningful and persuasive discourse.

Syntax is fundamentally the study of sentence structure or how words and phrases fit together to create coherent, grammatically accurate communication units. These linguistic elements adhere to conventions and practices that vary throughout languages rather than being arranged haphazardly. Grammar is the grammarian's toolbox; it helps us break down phrases into their constituent parts, comprehend how they relate, and create expressions that accurately represent our ideas.

The foundation of sentence construction lies in understanding the roles of critical syntactic elements. The focal point, or the thing behaving or being described, is the subject, usually a noun or pronoun. The verb, the engine of action or state of being, propels the sentence forward. On the other hand, the object either accepts the verb's action or enhances it. This basic Subject-Verb-Object (SVO) structure is a fundamental syntax pattern observed in languages as diverse as English, Mandarin, and Arabic.

Nevertheless, syntactic variation becomes apparent when considering languages departing from the SVO norm. Consider the Subject-Object-Verb (SOV) structure seen in Turkish and Japanese. In Japanese, "Watashi (I, subject) sushi (sushi, object) tabemasu (eat, verb)" presents a distinct syntactic order, emphasizing the object before the verb. This variation highlights how Syntax is flexible across languages, dispelling myths and demonstrating the variety of ways one can compose coherent sentences.

Syntax also embraces the concept of modifiers, elements that add detail, color, and nuance to the core components of a sentence. Adjectives, for instance, modify nouns, providing descriptive layers that enhance the richness of expression. In the sentence "The sun (noun) set (verb) behind the majestic mountains (adjective)," the adjective "majestic" paints a vivid picture, transforming a simple scene into a more evocative tableau. Like the Swiss army knives of Syntax, adverbs modify verbs, adjectives, or other adverbs, introducing nuances of time, manner, or degree. The use of adverbs in the sentence "She (subject) spoke (verb) eloquently" enhances the quality of speech and gives the sentence a more complex undertone.

Furthermore, clauses—groups of words with a subject and a verb that can stand alone or be included in a longer sentence—interact when building sentences. Independent clauses, capable of standing alone, form complete thoughts, while dependent clauses rely on independent clauses for coherence. Combining independent and dependent clauses allows for complex sentences where syntactic structures unfold like intricate origami, revealing layers of meaning and relationships.

The syntactic landscape further expands with the introduction of different sentence types. Declarative sentences make statements or express opinions, interrogative sentences pose questions, imperative sentences give commands, and exclamatory sentences convey strong emotions. The distinctive Syntax of each sentence type shapes the overall structure and influences the tone and communicative intent. The declarative "The sky is blue" adopts a straightforward syntax, while the interrogative "Is the sky blue?" reconfigures the word order to elicit information.

Punctuation, the unsung hero of Syntax, plays a crucial role in guiding readers through the syntactic maze. Navigational aids such as commas, periods, question marks, and exclamation points indicate pauses, stops, questions, or strong declarations. The syntactic dance gains rhythm and coherence through these punctuation markers, ensuring readers traverse the syntactic landscape with clarity and precision.

Syntax is not a static entity but a dynamic force that adapts to convey subtleties of meaning and cultural nuances. The passive voice is one grammatical shift that emphasizes the recipient of an action rather than the doer. In "The book (subject) was read (verb) by the student (agent)," the passive construction alters the traditional subject-verb-object order, highlighting the book rather than the student. This syntactic choice introduces variation in emphasis and tone, providing a nuanced tool for expression.

As demonstrated by the Syntax of honorifics in Korean and African-American English, cultural and geographical factors also shape Syntax. These differences show how language and society interact dynamically, with Syntax acting as a mirror to reflect social norms, values, and hierarchies. Syntax, in this context, transcends mere sentence construction; it becomes a cultural artifact, embodying the unique identity of a linguistic community.

Moreover, the study of Syntax encompasses psycholinguistics, investigating how the human mind interprets and utilizes syntactic patterns. According to research in this area, speakers of different languages may employ various cognitive methods when approaching Syntax, which reflects the linguistic patterns inherent in their mother tongues. The mental demands of deciphering intricate phrase forms highlight how the human brain adapts remarkably well to various syntactic environments.

In the digital age, Syntax also plays a role in natural language processing (NLP) and artificial intelligence. Comprehending syntactic patterns is essential for programming language models to interpret and produce writing that resembles that of humans. The intersection of Syntax with technology showcases the enduring relevance of linguistic principles in shaping advancements in communication and information processing.

To sum up, sentence structure and Syntax serve as the cornerstone of good communication, providing the means to create logical, complex, and expressive conversation. From basic sentence structures to the intricacies of clauses and modifiers, Syntax shapes how we organize words to convey meaning. The dynamic interplay of Syntax and culture reveals the profound connection between language and society. Far from being a rigid set of rules, Syntax emerges as an active and adaptive force, embodying the creativity and diversity inherent in human communication. As we proceed across the syntactic terrain, we reveal the creativity and adaptability that support the formation of meaningful conversation.

Syntax Variations Across Language Families

The beauty of language lies in the words we choose and the way we weave them together. Syntax, the structure that governs sentence formation, is a linguistic kaleidoscope reflecting the diversity of human communication. As we explore syntax variations across language families, we journey through the intricate patterns that shape the expression of meaning in different corners of the world.

A notable feature of syntax differences is the variety of word ordering in different language families. In the vast landscape of linguistic diversity, the Subject-Verb-Object (SVO) word order dominates in languages like English, Mandarin Chinese, and Swahili. In English, for instance, "The cat (subject) chased (verb) the mouse (object)" follows the SVO pattern, representing a standard structure familiar to speakers of many Indo-European languages. But we encounter exceptions to this rule when we move through language landscapes.

Languages such as Japanese and Turkish, belonging to the Altaic and Japonic language families, challenge the SVO convention by adopting a Subject-Object-Verb (SOV) word order. In Japanese, a sentence like "Watashi (I, subject) sushi (sushi, object) tabemasu (eat, verb)" structures information in a way that places the object before the verb. Similarly, Turkish sentences like "Ali (Ali, subject) Elma (apple, object) Jedi (ate, verb)" follow the SOV pattern. These variations demonstrate how languages can creatively arrange words to express meaning, going beyond the limitations of a particular word order paradigm and highlighting the versatility of Syntax.

Moreover, the syntactic diversity becomes even more pronounced when we delve into languages with Subject-Verb (SV) or Subject-Object (SO) structures. For instance, in Mandarin Chinese, a Subject-Verb structure is evident in sentences like "Wǒ (I, subject) chi (eat, verb)," where the object is often inferred from context or explicitly stated afterward. In contrast, languages like Persian or Arabic, belonging to the Afro-Asiatic language family, employ Subject-Object structures, as seen in sentences like "Ana (I, subject) Akala (ate, verb) tuffaha (apple, object)." These variations underscore the kaleidoscopic nature of Syntax, where different language families paint their unique patterns.

Another aspect of Syntax that adds to the richness of linguistic expression is case marks. Case marks alter nouns and pronouns in languages like German, Russian, and Latin to indicate grammatical relationships within a phrase. The accusative case, for instance, marks the direct object, as seen in the Latin sentence "Puella (girl, nominative) librum (book, accusative) legit (reads, verb)." In Russian, "Devushka (girl, nominative) chitaet (reads, verb) knife (book, accusative)" exhibits a similar case-marking pattern. Contrastingly, English, a Germanic language, relies more on word order and context to convey similar grammatical relationships, showcasing the syntactic diversity within language families.

Verbs, the engines of action and expression, also contribute to syntax variations. Romance languages like Spanish, French, and Italian are known for their rich verb conjugation systems, where verbs change forms to convey information about tense, mood, aspect, and person. For example, in Spanish, "Yo (I, subject) hablo (speak, verb)" indicates the present tense, while "Yo hablaba (I spoke)" reflects the past tense. English, a Germanic language, has a comparatively more straightforward verb conjugation system, often relying on auxiliary verbs and word order to convey temporal nuances.

Variations in Syntax are not limited to word order; they also affect social hierarchy and cultural values. In Korean and Japanese, Syntax is closely linked to social interactions and degrees of politeness. Different verb tenses and phrase constructions express different degrees of formality, reflecting cultural norms of hierarchy and respect. In Korean, the formal sentence "Jeoneun (I, subject) shaggy (school, object) ga (go, verb) imnida" contrasts with the informal "Na (I, subject) shaggy (school, object) ganda (go, verb)." These variations illustrate how Syntax becomes a cultural code intricately intertwined with social dynamics.

The treatment of gender in Syntax adds another layer to linguistic diversity. Grammatical gender is applied to nouns in Spanish and French, affecting agreement in articles and adjectives. The distinction between "el libro" (the book, masculine) and "la mesa" (the table, feminine) exemplifies how gender is embedded within the syntactic structure. In contrast, English, a language with minimal grammatical gender, relies more on pronouns and explicit markers to convey gender distinctions.

Furthermore, Syntax reflects historical and geographical factors, showcasing the evolution of languages over time. Creole languages were created.

Common Syntax Errors and How to Avoid Them

Syntax is the architectural framework in the intricate language landscape that gives structure and coherence to our expressions. Making grammatically correct sentences can be a challenging process, though. Common syntax errors, like hidden traps in the linguistic maze, can hinder effective communication. This exploration aims to shed light on some of these pitfalls and offer insights into how writers and speakers can navigate the intricacies of Syntax, ensuring clarity and precision in their communication.

One prevalent syntax error involves the misuse or omission of commas. Commas, often likened to traffic signals in the syntactic flow, guide readers through sentence pauses and separations.

Misplacing or omitting commas can lead to confusion and alter the intended meaning of a sentence. Take the difference between saying, "Let's eat, Grandma!" and "Let's eat, Grandma!" as an example. The placement of the comma distinguishes between an invitation to dine with Grandma and a potentially alarming suggestion. To avoid this error, writers should be mindful of the grammatical contexts that warrant commas, such as separating items in a list, setting off introductory phrases, or distinguishing between independent clauses.

A common syntactic pitfall is the misuse of pronouns, which can lead to ambiguity and confusion. Pronouns such as "he," "she," "it," or "they" are supposed to take the place of specific nouns in language to provide clarity and fluidity. However, the lack of clarity regarding the antecedent—the noun a pronoun replaces—can result in misunderstandings. In the statement "John told Bob that he lost his wallet," for example, it is not apparent who misplaced the wallet— John or Bob. It could be more noticeable to say, "John told Bob that Bob lost his wallet." Ensuring an unambiguous relationship between pronouns and their antecedents is crucial for effective communication.

Another syntactic challenge arises from faulty parallelism, a construction where similar elements within a sentence are not presented in a balanced or parallel structure. This error disrupts the rhythm and coherence of the sentence. Take the line "She likes to hike, swim, and ride a bike," for instance. The gerund form "hiking" and the infinitive phrase "to ride a bike" are mixed in an inconsistent construction that produces an unharmonious impression. Elaborating on the sentence to preserve parallelism, such as "She likes hiking, swimming, and biking," improves the syntactic harmony. When presenting comparable ideas within a sentence or listing items, writers must retain a parallel structure.

One grammatical element many authors need help with is subject-verb agreement, which leads to phrases with incorrect singular and plural forms. In English, the number of the subject and the verb of a sentence should match. For instance, the sentence "The team is playing well" should be corrected to "The team is playing well" to ensure agreement between the singular subject "team" and the singular verb "is." This error often occurs when intervening words or phrases separate the subject and verb. Maintaining agreement between subjects and verbs is essential for grammatical accuracy and coherence in sentence construction.

Refraining from using modifiers, including adjectives and adverbs, poses another syntax challenge. Modifiers enrich language by giving nouns and verbs more descriptive features. However, misplaced or dangling modifiers can lead to awkward and ambiguous constructions. As an illustration, the phrase "Riding the bicycle, the view impressed me" implies that the subject is cycling. A more apparent revision would be, "While riding the bicycle, I was impressed by the view." Writers must close modifiers to the words they want to change to prevent misunderstandings and preserve grammatical accuracy.

Sentence fragments and incomplete expressions presented as standalone sentences represent a syntactic error that disrupts the flow of ideas. Chips frequently lack a subject, a verb, or both elements needed to make a coherent concept. Take into consideration the passage "Although tired after the hike." To correct this, it should be expanded into a complete sentence, such as "Although tired after the hike, she felt a sense of accomplishment." Writers should be vigilant in constructing complete and grammatically sound sentences to convey coherent ideas and maintain syntactic integrity.

Run-on sentences present another syntactic hurdle, characterized by the absence of proper punctuation or conjunctions between independent clauses. These long phrases weaken the effect of individual ideas and may need to be clarified for readers. For instance, the run-on sentence "She enjoys hiking, she often goes on long trails" can be corrected using a conjunction or appropriate punctuation: "She enjoys hiking, and she often goes on long trails." Writers should be attentive to sentence boundaries and utilize punctuation or conjunctions to delineate distinct ideas.

Awkward wording is a grammatical problem that frequently occurs when writers aim for intricacy but unintentionally produce complex or ambiguous sentences. Syntax intricacy should be subordinated to clarity. For instance, the sentence "Because he was late, he missed the train" can be simplified to "Because he was late, he missed the train." Simplifying Syntax guarantees that readers can understand the intended meaning without needless complexity.

Inconsistent verb tense usage within a sentence or paragraph is a syntactic pitfall that can disrupt the temporal flow of ideas. Verb tenses should be used consistently by writers; avoid making needless changes that can confuse readers. For example, the sentence "She walked into the room, picked up a book, and started reading" can be revised for consistency: "She walked into the room, picked up a book, and started reading." Maintaining a consistent verb tense enhances the coherence and clarity of the syntactic structure.

Additionally, the misuse of conjunctions, such as "and," "but," or "or," can introduce syntactic errors, particularly in the context of compound sentences. Writers should ensure that conjunctions connect independent clauses of similar grammatical structure and maintain coherence. For instance, "She likes hiking, swimming, and riding a bike" can be corrected to "She likes hiking, swimming, and riding a bike" for syntactic accuracy and clarity.

To sum up, understanding typical hazards and the resources to avoid them is essential for navigating the complexities of Syntax. From commas to pronouns, parallelism to subject-verb agreement, writers must be attuned to the nuances of Syntax to construct clear, coherent, and grammatically sound sentences. By recognizing and avoiding these typical syntax errors, authors can boost the efficiency of their communication, ensuring that their thoughts are delivered with clarity and impact in the delicate fabric of language.

Practical Exercises for Syntax Mastery

In the intricate language landscape, mastering Syntax is akin to acquiring the keys to a complex code that governs the arrangement of words and phrases, shaping the very fabric of communication. Whether you're a budding writer, a student honing your linguistic skills, or someone passionate about language nuances, practical exercises for syntax mastery are invaluable tools. These tasks help you grasp Syntax more deeply and allow you to apply its rules with skill. This investigation explores a range of useful functions for different ability levels, enabling a path to syntactic proficiency.

At the foundational level, sentence construction exercises offer an excellent starting point. Crafting sentences with precision requires a grasp of basic syntactic structures. Start with basic phrases and concentrate on the subjects, verbs, and objects—the three main components. Create sentences using the Subject-Verb-Object (SVO) pattern, for example. Explore variants like Subject-Object-Verb (SOV) or Subject-Verb (SV) as you get more comfortable. This progression builds a solid syntactic foundation, reinforcing the fundamental structures that underpin more complex linguistic expressions.

Phrase-combining activities provide a dynamic syntax-mastering approach beyond simple phrase formation. You are asked to combine two or more simple sentences into a single, coherent sentence for these assignments. This improves your comprehension of language structure and fosters original thought when expressing ideas. Consider the following sentence: "The sun was setting." The sky took on pink and orange tones." Combining these sentences could result in "As the sun set, the sky transformed into hues of pink and orange." Such exercises foster an appreciation for syntactic variety and encourage the exploration of diverse sentence structures.

As you move on to increasingly complex tasks, syntactic analysis exercises provide a thorough understanding of sentence patterns. Selected complex sentences from books or articles should be broken down into their constituent clauses, phrases, and modifiers. This analytical approach sharpens your ability to recognize syntactic patterns and understand how they contribute to meaning. Additionally, these exercises cultivate a critical eye for syntactic nuances, enabling you to apply similar intricacies in your writing.

Exploring different syntactic structures is essential for comprehensive syntax mastery. For example, parallelism activities test your ability to construct balanced phrases. Ensure the sentence's components are aligned and have consistent grammatical forms. This polishes your syntactic skills and cultivates a sense of rhythm and flow in your writing. For instance, construct sentences like "She enjoys hiking, swimming, and reading," where each element follows a parallel structure, enhancing syntactic harmony.

Another effective exercise involves manipulating word order to convey different emphases within a sentence. Try altering the parts of a simple statement to see how the focus changes. Start an account, for instance, with "The cat caught the mouse." By altering the word order to "The mouse was caught by the cat" or "Caught by the cat, the mouse scurried away," you gain insights into how syntactic choices influence the focus and tone of a sentence. This practice gives you a sophisticated grasp of Syntax for meaning transmission.

Syntactic variety exercises encourage experimentation with diverse sentence structures. Try writing sentences with a variety of lengths, designs, and styles. This gives your text more depth and improves your syntactic flexibility. For instance, juxtapose a short, declarative sentence with a longer, complex one to create a dynamic rhythm.

These exercises foster creativity and help you break free from syntactic monotony.

Incorporating syntactic devices into your writing is a crucial aspect of mastery. For example, anaphora exercises encourage you to employ repetition for rhetorical effect. Create sentences or paragraphs that begin each subsequent clause or sentence with the same word or phrase. This enhances stylistic refinement in addition to adding focus. Take the following example: "She discovered serenity in the garden." There, in the garden, she found beauty. In the garden, she unearthed secrets." This practice improves your command of grammar as a persuasive device.

From individual sentences to larger discourse units, syntactic fluency exercises involve writing passages or short stories focusing on diverse sentence structures. Try to use a variety of phrase structures, lengths, and levels of complexity. This exercise reinforces syntactic mastery and prepares you to handle the complexities of longer-form writing. It lets you easily switch between grammatical structures, keeping your writing exciting and lively.

Exerting yourself in phrase transformation tasks helps you improve your syntactic abilities. Take a sentence and challenge yourself to express the same idea using different syntactic structures. This task challenges you to consider how the system affects style and meaning. For example, transform the sentence "The tree stood tall" into "Tall and imposing, the tree dominated the landscape" or "The tall tree dominated the landscape." These drills help you develop your syntactic repertoire's adaptability.

Beyond written exercises, oral practice is equally valuable for syntax mastery. Take part in conversations or activities where you must develop sentences on the spot. This real-time application of syntactic knowledge enhances your ability to think syntactically on your feet. Oral exercises reinforce syntactic principles and contribute to overall language fluency.

Modern technology provides creative syntactic practice opportunities. Use internet resources and apps for language learning that offer interactive activities according to your skill level. These tools frequently provide immediate feedback, letting you monitor your development and pinpoint improvement areas. Using technology in your syntactic practice regimen gives your learning process a dynamic and exciting twist.

Peer review exercises also provide a cooperative method of mastering Syntax. Collaborate with classmates on written assignments and offer helpful criticism on grammatical errors. Analyzing other people's writing strengthens editing and identifying different grammatical patterns. By encouraging a community of learners, this reciprocal process creates a conducive atmosphere for syntactic exploration and development.

In summary, the foundation of efficient language use is a grasp of Syntax through practical activities. These activities provide an all-encompassing approach to mastering Syntax, ranging from essential sentence building to complex syntactic analysis, and they are designed to accommodate a variety of skill levels. By engaging in diverse exercises encompassing written, oral, and digital modalities, you deepen your understanding of Syntax and cultivate a versatile and dynamic command over the nuances of language. As you navigate the linguistic landscape through these exercises, you embark on a journey toward syntactic mastery, unlocking the intricate code that shapes meaningful communication.

Chapter III

The Road to Semantics

Introduction to Semantics

In linguistics, semantics emerges as a captivating field that delves into the intricate dance of meaning within language. While syntax governs the structure of sentences, semantics navigates the nuanced landscape of importance, exploring how words and expressions convey ideas, concepts, and emotions. This introduction to semantics unravels the tapestry of meaning, shedding light on the fundamental concepts that underpin this fascinating linguistic discipline.

Semantics is fundamentally the study of language meaning. It looks at how a word's arrangement affects the entire meaning of a linguistic phrase, going beyond only word choice. Semantics offers the instruments to comprehend, evaluate, and interpret the meaning that spoken or written language conveys. From the subtle nuances of individual words to the broader context in which they exist, semantics explores the layers of meaning that give the language its richness and depth.

One of the foundational concepts in semantics is linguistic signs, which consists of the relationship between a signifier (the form a word or expression takes) and its signified (the concept or meaning it represents). This relationship, often attributed to the Swiss linguist Ferdinand de Saussure, highlights the arbitrariness of the connection between a word's sound or written form and its meaning. For example, the English word "dog" bears no inherent connection to the furry, four-legged animal it represents; the association is purely conventional and agreed upon within a linguistic community.

Semantics studies how words refer to things in the real world, challenging the idea of reference. The relationship between words and the things, activities, or concepts they refer to is known as reference. In this context, semantics distinguishes between different types of reference, including direct reference (where a word directly points to an object, as in "the Eiffel Tower") and indirect reference (where a term refers to something through description or association, as in "the tallest building in Paris"). Understanding reference is essential for unraveling the layers of meaning embedded in language.

The study of semantics extends to the examination of sense, a term that captures the unique meaning or concept associated with a word in a given context. The different shades of meaning a comment can have and how these meanings interact with other words in particular linguistic settings are all included. For example, the term "bank" might describe the side of a river, a financial organization, or the action of tilting one way or the other. The context in which the word "bank" is employed shapes its meaning, demonstrating how purpose is dynamic and context-dependent.

Polysemy and homonymy are two phenomena within semantics that add complexity to the study of meaning. A scenario known as polysemy occurs when a single word has several related meanings. Think that the term "bat" may refer to a flying animal and an item of sporting goods. There is an underlying principle that unites these meanings. Conversely, homophones are terms that have the exact spelling but different meanings. An example is the word "bank," which, as mentioned earlier, can refer to a financial institution or the side of a river. Distinguishing between polysemy and homonymy is crucial for understanding the nuances of meaning ambiguity in language.

In addition to examining individual word meanings, semantics explores the intricate dance of meaning within sentences and larger discourse units. Sentence semantics involves understanding how the meaning of individual words combines to create the overall meaning of a sentence. Semantic roles, which designate distinct parts for various sentence components, are studied during this procedure. In the sentence "John ate the apple," for instance, "John" refers to the agent acting, "ate" to the activity, and "the apple" to the theme—the thing that the action affects. Semantic roles contribute to the coherence and clarity of sentences, allowing us to decipher the relationships between different elements.

Semantics goes beyond the level of sentences into pragmatics, a closely related discipline that studies how context shapes meaning. Pragmatics recognizes that the interpretation of linguistic expressions often relies on shared knowledge, social conventions, and situational context. The exact words spoken in different contexts can carry vastly different meanings. Think about the phrase, "Can you pass the salt?" The underlying assumption behind this straightforward request is that salt is frequently used as a condiment when eating. Pragmatic considerations enrich our understanding of meaning by acknowledging the role of context in shaping interpretation.

Studying truth conditions and truth-conditional semantics is an essential component of semantics. According to this method, a sentence's meaning is directly related to the circumstances determining whether it is accurate or untrue. For example, if a cat is placed on a mat in a specific location, the statement "The cat is on the mat" is factual. Truth-conditional semantics connects linguistic expressions to the status of the world by offering a systematic approach to the analysis and representation of sentence meaning.

Semantics is concerned with the meaning of words and sentences and the broader concepts of sense relations and semantic fields. Sense relations investigate the semantic relationships between words. Common sense relations include synonymy, hyponymy, hypernymy, and antonymy. "Hot" and "cold" are examples of antonyms, which are words with opposing meanings. Words that seem similar, like "happy" and "joyful," are synonyms. Hyponyms are words that represent more specific instances of a general concept (e.g., "rose" is a hyponym of "flower"). In contrast, hypernyms represent broader categories (e.g., "fruit" is a hypernym of "apple"). Understanding these sense relations illuminates the semantic landscape and enriches our grasp of language interconnectedness.

Lexical semantics, concerned with the meaning of individual words, and compositional semantics, which looks at how the meaning of more significant language expressions is constructed from the meanings of its component pieces, are two areas in which semantics research intersect. Understanding how words fit together syntactically and semantically to produce complex meanings is known as compositional semantics. For instance, the meaning of the phrase "big red ball" is not simply the sum of its word meanings but involves the interaction and integration of these meanings. Compositional semantics provides tools for unraveling the complexity of meaning in phrases and sentences.

Semantics presents a comprehensive framework for comprehending meaning; nonetheless, it faces several obstacles and disagreements. The question of linguistic relativity, often associated with the Sapir-Whorf hypothesis, explores whether a language's structure influences how its speakers perceive and think about the world. While some argue that language shapes thought, others emphasize the universality of specific cognitive processes. Additionally, debates persist about the nature of meaning and whether a referential or conceptual approach best captures it. These ongoing discussions contribute to the dynamic and evolving nature of semantic theory.

To sum up, semantics offers a fascinating exploration of the core of meaning in language. Semantics reveals the nuances of sense, polysemy, pragmatics, and basic notions of language signs and references that form the structure of human communication. We get a deep knowledge of how language creates and communicates meaning as we traverse the fields of truth-conditional semantics, sense relations, and compositional semantics. Semantics equips us with the tools to analyze linguistic expressions and invites us to appreciate the dynamic interplay of words, senses, and contexts.

Meaning and Significance

Language's meaning and significance are fundamental components within the complex human communication network. Individuals constantly dance with words to weave elaborate narratives that convey our thoughts, feelings, and experiences. This exploration delves into the profound realms of meaning and significance, unravelling the threads that weave together the fabric of our linguistic existence.

Meaning is fundamentally the lifeblood of language; it is the dynamic power that converts intelligible sounds or written symbols into communication channels. It bridges our thoughts and the external world, allowing us to convey, share, and comprehend complex concepts. Semantics, the study of meaning, examines the complex connections between words, their forms, and the ideas they stand for. It goes beyond syntax, or how sentences are put together, to investigate the minute details and gradations of meaning in certain words and phrases.

Linguistic signs, a fundamental concept in semantics, encapsulate the relationship between the form a word takes (the signifier) and the concept or meaning it represents (the signified). This relationship, as postulated by Ferdinand de Saussure, underlines the arbitrariness of the link between a word's sound or written form and its meaning. For example, the term "tree" has nothing to do with the tall, green thing it represents. Instead, the association emerges from convention, a mutual understanding among speakers of the same language.

Reference, a cornerstone of semantics, delves into the connection between words and the entities or ideas they point to in the world. Comprehending relation is similar to reading the map connecting language and reality. Direct contact involves a word meaning an object, such as "the Statue of Liberty." At the same time, indirect reference relies on description or association, as seen in "The Tallest Mountain in the World." Connection serves as a compass for us as we navigate the world of meaning, enabling words to go beyond linguistic bounds and touch on our everyday life's material and immaterial facets.

Sensation, a subtle aspect of meaning, captures the particular purpose or idea connected to a word in a specific situation. It encompasses the various dimensions a comment can assume, revealing the kaleidoscope of meanings that emerge based on the surrounding linguistic landscape. Consider the word "run," for instance. Its sense can shift from a physical activity to a malfunction in a system, showcasing the malleability of meaning within the fluidity of context. Comprehending reason is like navigating the changing colours of a language painting, where every brushstroke adds to the final beauty.

Polysemy and homonymy introduce layers of complexity to the study of meaning. Polysemy refers to the phenomenon where a single word has multiple related meanings. For example, "bat" can refer to a flying animal or a piece of athletic gear, and a common idea relates both meanings. On the other hand, homonymy involves words that share the same form but have distinct meanings. Distinguishing between polysemy and homonymy illuminates language's intricate dance of ambiguity and specificity.

Semantics extends its gaze beyond the microcosm of individual words to the macrocosm of sentences and discourse. Sentence semantics explores how the meaning of individual words combines to create the overarching significance of a sentence. It is vital to look at semantic roles, which provide different sentence elements with specific purposes. Semantic roles clarify the connections between various components and improve the coherence and understandability of sentences.

A related discipline to semantics, pragmatics explores shared knowledge and context. It acknowledges that meaning is not solely derived from individual words or sentence structures but is profoundly influenced by the situational and cultural context in which communication occurs. The statement "Can you pass the salt?" gains its whole meaning from the words themselves and the shared knowledge that salt is a common condiment used during meals. By acknowledging the interaction between language and context—where words get meaning from the fabric of shared experiences—pragmatics deepens our comprehension of meaning.

Sentence meaning can be systematically analyzed and represented using truth conditions and truth-conditional semantics. According to this approach, the importance of a sentence is intimately tied to the conditions under which it would be considered true or false. For instance, the sentence "The sun rises in the east" is true if, in a given context, the sun rises in the east. Truth-conditional semantics bridges language and reality, offering a systematic means to understand how linguistic expressions correspond to states of affairs.

Sense relations and semantic fields broaden the exploration of meaning by examining how words relate to one another. The relationships between words with opposite meanings (like "hot" and "cold") and between words with similar meanings (like "happy" and "joyful"), known as Antonymy and synonymy, respectively, demonstrate the complex network of relationships that exist within language. Hyponymy and hypernymy further illustrate how words nestle within broader or narrower categories, enriching our understanding of the hierarchical structure of meaning. Sense relations show how words are related to one another and the semantic fields that establish meaning's boundaries.

The perspectives of lexical semantics and compositional semantics are complementary for examining meaning. The study of lexical semantics delves into the meaning of individual words, revealing the various aspects of a single lexical entry. Compositional semantics, on the other hand, investigates how the importance of particular words combines syntactically and semantically to create complex meanings in phrases and sentences. Combined, these methods provide an extensive arsenal for analyzing the subtle differences in meaning between various language units.

Although semantics is fundamental to comprehending meaning in language, there are always discussions and difficulties around it. The question of linguistic relativity, associated with the Sapir-Whorf hypothesis, explores whether a language's structure influences how its speakers perceive and think about the world. While some argue for the shaping influence of language on thought, others emphasize the universality of specific cognitive processes. There are also ongoing disagreements concerning whether a referential or conceptual approach better captures the essence of linguistic significance and debates concerning the nature of meaning itself. These discussions highlight how semantic theory is a living, breathing concept.

In conclusion, meaning and significance form the beating heart of human expression, breathing life into language and allowing us to navigate the complexities of communication. From the foundational concepts of linguistic signs and reference to the nuanced exploration of sense, polysemy, and pragmatics, semantics unravels the layers of meaning that constitute the fabric of our linguistic existence. We get a deep understanding of the complex dance of words, senses, and contexts that creates the mosaic of meaning in our shared human experience as we navigate truth-conditional semantics, sense relations, and the junction of lexical and compositional semantics.

Semantic Fields and Relations

Semantics acts as the cartographer, mapping the intricate landscape of meaning in the vast expanse of language, where words serve as vessels for ideas, emotions, and experiences. Within this terrain, semantic fields and relations emerge as dynamic tools illuminating the interconnectedness of terms and their shades of significance. This exploration delves into the profound intricacies of semantic domains and links, unraveling the layers that contribute to the richness of language.

Semantic fields, often likened to the interconnected branches of a linguistic tree, represent the thematic clusters of words that share a common conceptual domain. These fields form a tapestry that weaves together words related by their meanings, creating a network of associations that enrich our understanding of language. For instance, within the semantic field of "emotion," words like "joy," "sorrow," and "anger" nestle together, each contributing a distinct hue to the broader canvas of emotional experience. Semantic fields are cognitive maps that lead us across language's thematic landscapes, revealing connections between words and subtle differences within particular areas.

A branch of semantics called sense relations enables us to investigate the complex relationships between words in a semantic field, expanding our understanding of semantics. Antonymy, perhaps the most familiar sense relation, manifests in the opposition between words with opposite meanings. The anonymous pair "hot" and "cold" exemplify this relationship, as the contrasting concepts create a dynamic tension within the semantic field of temperature. Conversely, synonymy shows terms with related meanings, like "happy" and "joyful," which enhances the language's vitality and expressiveness. These sense relations offer a microscope through which we can examine the nuances and shades within a semantic field, highlighting the subtle distinctions and relationships that give depth to our linguistic expressions.

A hierarchical aspect to semantic linkages is added by hyponymy and hypernymy, which show how words fit into larger or smaller categories. Hyponyms represent specific instances or subcategories within a general concept, while hypernyms encompass the overarching category that includes these subcategories. For example, in the semantic field, "flowers," "rose," and "daisy" are hyponyms, referring to certain kinds of flowers, whereas "flower" is the hypernym, referring to the larger category. By adding a layer of order to semantic fields, this hierarchical structure makes it easier for us to navigate the taxonomies that support our conceptual knowledge of reality.

Understanding the dynamic interplay of sense relations within a semantic field requires an exploration of antonymy, a sense relation that encapsulates the opposition between words with opposite meanings. Antonyms, such as "happy" and "sad" or "big" and "small," create a spectrum within the semantic field, showcasing the polarities that define certain concepts. This oppositional relationship improves our capacity to communicate minute differences in meaning and add to various expressions. Within the semantic field of "temperature," the antonymic pair "hot" and "cold" exemplify this dynamic relationship, allowing us to articulate the range of thermal experiences.

Another essential sense relation called synonymy sheds light on words with comparable meanings, enhancing the language's adaptability and subtlety. Synonyms offer alternatives for expressive variation, enabling speakers and writers to tailor their linguistic choices to specific contexts. For example, within the semantic field of "intelligence," synonyms like "smart," "clever," and "wise" provide nuanced shades of meaning, allowing for precise and contextually appropriate expressions. Synonymy enriches language by offering a spectrum of options within a semantic field, facilitating precision in communication and enhancing the stylistic palette available to language users.

A hierarchical component is added to sense relations by hyponymy and hypernymy, which clarify how words relate to one another within larger or smaller categories. Hyponyms represent specific instances or subcategories within a general concept, while hypernyms encompass the overarching category that includes these subcategories. Within the semantic domain of "vehicles," "car" and "bicycle," for instance, are synonyms.

By adding a layer of structure to semantic fields, this hierarchical organization enables us to understand the taxonomies that are ingrained in our conception of reality.

Semantic fields and relations extend beyond the realms of individual words to influence larger discourse units. Examining how meaning is created and communicated throughout lengthy linguistic segments, like paragraphs, conversations, or narratives, is the focus of discourse semantics. Coherent devices, such as pronouns, conjunctions, and lexical repetitions, enhance a speech's coherence and unity of meaning. The cohesive ties within a text create a semantic network that guides readers or listeners through the flow of ideas, ensuring a coherent and understandable experience.

Exploring the dynamics of semantic fields and relations invites us to delve into the multifaceted nature of language. Polysemy, a phenomenon where a single word has multiple related meanings, adds a layer of complexity to semantic analysis. For instance, "bank" can describe a financial institution and the bank itself, demonstrating how similar language forms can have different meanings. The power of words to change and alter their meanings depending on usage and context is highlighted by polysemy.

Contrary to polysemy, homology refers to words with identical forms but different meanings. Homonyms can lead to semantic ambiguity, as the same word shape conceals other underlying concepts. For instance, there may be misunderstandings when using the term "bat," which can relate to both a flying mammal and an item of sporting goods. Making the distinction between polysemy and homophones advances our knowledge of how words originate and convey meaning in various linguistic circumstances.

Exploring semantic fields and relations also intersects with lexical semantics, the study of the meaning of individual words. Lexical semantics dives into the various dimensions of meaning encapsulated within a single word, unraveling the intricacies that contribute to its semantic profile. This granular analysis enhances our understanding of how words operate within specific semantic fields and the subtle nuances they introduce to language.

Compositional semantics, a complementary perspective, examines how the meanings of individual words combine syntactically and semantically to create complex definitions in phrases and sentences.

Understanding how words combine to produce substances that are more than the sum of their parts is known as compositional semantics. For instance, the phrase "big red ball" involves the interaction of three words, each contributing a distinct aspect.

Semantics Across Cultures

Language, as a fundamental tool for human expression, is a dynamic tapestry woven with cultural threads. Within this intricate mosaic, semantics—the study of meaning—takes on new dimensions when traversing the diverse landscapes of different cultures. The nuanced dance of words, the subtleties of expression, and the layers of meaning are deeply intertwined with cultural contexts. This investigation explores the rich fabric of semantics across cultural boundaries, recognizing the significant impact of cultural variety on our understanding, communication, and interpretation of meaning.

At the heart of semantics across cultures lies the recognition that language is not a neutral vessel for universal concepts but a vibrant reflection of cultural worldviews. Words carry the imprints of cultural experiences, values, and perspectives, shaping their meanings. Consider the Japanese word "wa," which symbolizes the harmonic cohesion of a society, or the incomprehensible German phrase "Schadenfreude," which conveys happiness at the suffering of others. These statements that are peculiar to cultures highlight distinct aspects of the human experience and show how meaning is intricately entwined with cultural settings.

Semantic differences between cultures cover more than words and entire linguistic frameworks. One example of how cultural subtleties shape communication is seen in the way languages encode politeness. In Japanese, using honorifics, such as "san" or "sama," reflects a deeply ingrained respect for hierarchy and social roles. Conversely, languages like English may rely on intonation or indirect expressions to convey politeness. Understanding these cultural intricacies is essential for effective cross-cultural communication, as misinterpreting the politeness markers in a language can lead to unintended misunderstandings.

Idiomatic expressions, a rich source of cultural semantics, further illuminate the cultural nuances embedded in language. Idioms are often deeply rooted in cultural metaphors, historical events, or local customs. For instance, the English expression "raining cats and dogs" makes little sense outside its cultural context, highlighting the peculiarities contributing to the richness of meaning within a language. Examining colloquial language from various cultural contexts opens the door to comprehending the distinctive ways that other communities interpret and communicate universal human experiences.

The influence of cultural semantics extends to the very structure of languages. The grammatical encoding of concepts varies among languages, reflecting cultural values and viewpoints. Anthropologist Edward T. Hall distinguished between "high-context" and "low-context" civilizations; this idea is essential for comprehending how cultural semantics influence communication techniques. High-context cultures, such as those in East Asia, rely on implicit cues, shared knowledge, and context for meaning, while low-context cultures, like those in North America, prioritize explicit verbal expression. These differences highlight the complex interactions between language, culture, and meaning formation.

Color semantics offers a striking example of how cultural viewpoints shape language classifications. The color spectrum is divided into many categories by many civilizations, affecting how colors are named and how they are viewed and connected to feelings or meanings. For example, the Himba people of Namibia have different color classifications than what Western languages may combine. This cultural-specific color perception challenges the notion of a universal understanding of colors, revealing the cultural subjectivity that permeates even seemingly objective aspects of language.

The Sapir-Whorf hypothesis, often distilled into the ideas of linguistic relativity, posits that language influences thought. While the strong form of this hypothesis, suggesting that language determines thought, is debated, there is a consensus that language shapes our cognitive processes and influences how we conceptualize the world. Cultural semantics is essential to this interaction since language's subtleties affect how we perceive the world, make decisions, and comprehend it. For example, the Navajo language's intricate system of spatial relations has been shown to influence speakers' spatial cognition, challenging the idea of a universal, culture-independent cognitive framework.

The cultural semantics of time provides another fascinating lens through which to explore linguistic relativity. Different cultures conceptualize and express time in varied ways, influencing language and cognitive processes related to temporal orientation. While

English speakers often conceptualize time as linear and progress-oriented (e.g., "looking forward to the future" or "putting the past behind us"), cultures like the Aymara in South America may view time as flowing from the past in front of them to the future behind them. These culturally specific temporal frameworks show how language, cognition, and cultural views of time interact in complex ways.

Metaphors, deeply ingrained in language, offer a gateway to understanding cultural semantics by revealing how abstract concepts are grounded in concrete, culturally specific imagery. For example, there are cultural differences in the metaphorical language used to discuss time. English speakers frequently use phrases like "saving time" or "spending time," but Mandarin Chinese speakers could employ analogies that refer to the accrual or depletion of time as a resource. These cultural metaphors influence people's conceptualization and relationship to abstract notions in addition to shaping language expressions.

Semantic intercultural analysis extends beyond language structures to pragmatic communication characteristics. Pragmatics, the study of language use in context, recognizes that interpreting linguistic expressions relies on shared knowledge, social conventions, and situational context. Politeness strategies, speech registers, and conversational norms vary across cultures, influencing how communicative acts are perceived and interpreted. Please grasp these pragmatic nuances to avoid misunderstandings, as seen in cross-cultural interactions where politeness markers or indirect communication styles may be misconstrued.

Translational semantic changes highlight the cultural complexity of meaning even more. Translating between languages involves finding equivalent words and navigating the cultural baggage and connotations carried by those words. The cultural subtleties that shaped the original meaning could be lost in a word-for-word translation. For instance, the Portuguese word "saudade" connotes a nuanced blend of melancholy, desire, and nostalgia.

Chapter IV

Semantic Analysis

Understanding Word Meanings

As a vessel for human communication, language is a tapestry woven with words, each carrying layers of meaning shaped by context, usage, and cultural nuances. Lexical semantics, or the study of word meanings, is crucial to understanding the intricacies of language. This investigation explores the complex relationship between words and the rich tapestry of associations, connotations, and subtleties they add to our language expression. It also looks at the varied terrain of word meaning comprehension.

Lexical semantics begins its journey by acknowledging that the meaning of a word extends beyond a mere dictionary definition. Every word has a semantic payload, connections, feelings, and situational details that add to its meaning. For example, the word "home" might conjure up sentiments of coziness, acceptance, or fond memories that go beyond a dictionary's succinct description of a place to live. Navigating this semantic terrain, where the collision of personal and collective experiences influences how words resonate with speakers and listeners, is necessary to understand word meanings.

The concept of a word's denotation and connotation forms a cornerstone of lexical semantics. Denotation refers to a word's literal, primary meaning—the objective and universally agreed-upon definition found in dictionaries. Connotation, conversely, encompasses the additional layers of meaning, emotions, or associations that a word carries, often shaped by cultural, social, or personal contexts. Think about the term "snake." While its denotation refers to a legless, slithering reptile, the connotations may include ideas of deceit, danger, or temptation, influenced by cultural symbolism and individual experiences.

Semantic fields, intricate networks of related words that cluster around a central theme, further enrich our understanding of word meanings. These domains establish a semantic community in which words have similar conceptual underpinnings. Upon examining the semantic field of "family," one can uncover a plethora of terms such as "parent," "sibling," and "home," all of which offer distinct nuances of interpretation to the overall subject matter. Semantic fields provide a contextual framework that allows us to appreciate the nuanced relationships between words and how they collectively shape our understanding of broader concepts.

Sense relations within lexical semantics unravel the intricate connections between words, illuminating how they relate within the semantic field. Antonymy, the relationship between words with opposite meanings, introduces a dynamic tension that enhances the expressive range of language. Words like "happy" and "sad" form an antonymous pair, creating a spectrum within the semantic field of emotions. Synonymy, in contrast, brings words with similar meanings into dialogue, allowing for subtle variations in expression. Synonyms like "joyful" and "content" coexist within the semantic field of positive emotions, offering a nuanced palette for articulating specific shades of meaning.

Hyponymy and hypernymy add a hierarchical dimension to sense relations, delineating the relationships between specific instances and overarching categories. Subcategories that fall under a more significant notion or hypernym are represented by hyponyms. Within the semantic field of "fruit," for example, "apple" and "banana" are hyponyms, or particular kinds of fruit, and "fruit" is the hypernym that refers to all types of fruit. Understanding these hierarchical relationships enhances our ability to navigate the taxonomies inherent in lexical semantics, revealing the layered structure underpinning our world conceptualization.

Polysemy and homonymy introduce layers of complexity to word meanings. When a term has several related meanings, usually linked by a common underlying concept, this is referred to as polysemy. For instance, the word "bank" can refer to both the side of a river and a financial organization, demonstrating the flexibility and adaptation of word meanings. Homonymy, in contrast, involves words that share the same form but have distinct meanings. The term "bat" can describe both a flying mammal and a piece of sporting equipment, demonstrating the ambiguity inherent in language. Navigating polysemy and homonymy requires an acute awareness of context and usage to discern the intended meaning in specific instances.

Cultural semantics significantly shape word meanings since language is intricately entwined with cultural norms, beliefs, and experiences. Words often carry cultural connotations and evoke specific artistic imagery. For instance, the term "freedom" may evoke different associations and emotions in the contexts of American and Chinese cultures, reflecting the cultural values embedded in the word's meaning. Exploring word meanings within a cultural context broadens our understanding of the nuanced interplay between language and culture, where words become vessels for shared values and experiences.

Semantic shifts in translation further highlight the cultural complexities of word meanings. Translating between languages involves finding equivalent words and navigating the cultural baggage and connotations carried by those words. The cultural subtleties that shaped the original meaning could be lost in a word-for-word translation. For instance, it is difficult to translate the Portuguese word "saudade" into English since it encapsulates a nuanced blend of nostalgia, longing, and melancholy. The richness of word meanings is intricately tied to cultural contexts, and effective translation requires an awareness of the cultural resonances embedded in words.

Words can create mental images and influence perceptions. The field of cognitive semantics explores how words affect thought processes and mental representations. Metaphors, deeply ingrained in language, offer a lens through which we conceptualize abstract concepts by relating them to concrete, often culturally specific, experiences. For example, cultural metaphors about the passage of time are reflected in the varied metaphorical terms used when discussing time. This intersection of language, cognition, and culture underscores the intricate relationship between word meanings and the mental frameworks through which we interpret the world.

In conclusion, understanding word meanings is a journey through a rich and intricate landscape, where denotation, connotation, semantic fields, sense relations, and cultural nuances converge to shape the multifaceted meanings of words. Explore the dynamic interactions between words and the rich tapestry of associations and connotations they bring to our language expression via the lens of lexical semantics. It explores the live, changing character of language as a mirror of human cognition, culture, and experience that goes beyond the bounds of dictionaries.

Ambiguity in Language

One fascinating aspect of language, the complex fabric of human communication, is its intrinsic ambiguity. The exact words, phrases, or sentences can unfurl an array of meanings, leading to both delight and frustration in our attempts to convey and interpret messages. Ambiguity is a pervasive and multifaceted aspect of language, and this exploration delves into the labyrinth of multiple meanings, unraveling the intricacies of how wording invites, confounds, and adapts to the nuanced dance of interpretation.

Ambiguity results from language's natural capacity for adaptation and flexibility. As symbols of meaning, words frequently have several meanings or shades of interpretation. The phenomenon of polysemy, in which a single word has multiple connected meanings, is an example of this linguistic adaptability. Consider the term "bank," which can be used to describe a financial organization, the bank of a river, or even an aviation maneuver. Each meaning is distinct yet connected, highlighting the dynamic nature of language as it accommodates a spectrum of interpretations within a single lexical entry.

Homonymy adds another degree of ambiguity by using terms with similar forms but distinct meanings. These homophones can cause amusing wordplay and confusion. The word "bat," which may refer to a flying mammal and a piece of baseball equipment, is a prime example. The ambiguity of homonyms tests our ability to reason by forcing us to infer intended meanings from usage and context.

Ambiguity is not limited to single words but includes syntactic and sentence formations. Structural ambiguity arises when the arrangement of words allows for multiple interpretations. One classic instance is "I saw the man with the telescope." Does it mean the speaker observed a man with a telescope, or does it imply the speaker used a telescope to see a man from a distance? The syntactic structure opens the door to different interpretations, highlighting the role of context and pragmatic cues in disambiguating meaning.

Conversely, semantic ambiguity results from some words or expressions' innate imprecision or vagueness. Words with vague bounds, such as "soon," "many," or "good," require context to be understood. For example, saying "We need more time" creates uncertainty about how long "more time" means. Without additional context, the statement remains open to varied interpretations, allowing listeners to fill in the temporal gaps based on their assumptions or expectations.

Ambiguity is a powerful technique used in many types of artistic expression, not just a linguistic oddity. The complexity of ambiguous language often fosters the best writing in poetry, comedy, and literature. Unclear Sentences or phrases might pique readers' or listeners' interest by encouraging them to participate in the interpretation process. Ambiguity is a literary device, an emotional trigger, and a tool to help artists and authors create works that speak to various audiences. It encourages a dynamic exchange between the artist and the viewer in which interpretation is a collaborative process that co-creates meaning.

In humor, ambiguity serves as a wellspring of wit and wordplay. Puns, a classic form of linguistic humor, rely on words' dual meanings or sounds to create a humorous effect. The way the word "flies" creates an intriguing ambiguity in the line "Time flies like an arrow; fruit flies like a banana" signifies a beautiful illustration of how language can be humorous. The unexpected makes things funny, and ambiguity is a great place to create comic surprises with language tricks.

While ambiguity offers artistic and creative possibilities, it also poses challenges in legal and technical domains where precision is paramount. Legal documents, contracts, and technical manuals require unambiguous language to clarify and prevent misunderstandings. The ambiguity of a phrase in an agreement could lead to legal disputes, emphasizing the need for meticulous drafting to eliminate potential loopholes. In technical fields, precise and unambiguous language is crucial for accurately conveying instructions, specifications, and safety guidelines.

However, ambiguity is not always a barrier that needs to be surmounted; it can be a helpful instrument in strategic communication. Deliberate ambiguity, often employed in diplomacy or negotiation, allows speakers to navigate sensitive situations by leaving room for multiple interpretations. With their deliberate ambiguity, diplomatic statements allow for some flexibility and allow parties to establish a middle ground without committing to a particular stance. The intentional use of ambiguity highlights language's strategic aspect, where relationships are greatly influenced by the things left unsaid.

Disambiguating language is greatly aided by context, which provides guidance for readers or listeners as they negotiate the terrain of interpretation. The study of pragmatics, or language use in context, acknowledges that situational and cultural elements significantly impact meaning and that meaning is not only obtained from linguistic forms. The need for cooperation and context in resolving ambiguity is highlighted by Grice's Maxims, which are principles of conversational implicature. For example, the Maxim of Relation emphasizes relevance to the context, whereas the Maxim of Quantity advocates offering enough information for communication without being overly verbose. Recognizing and putting these maxims into practice reduces ambiguity and promotes ordinary meaning, which improves communication.

Differences in culture contribute yet another level of ambiguity's intricacy. In one culture, anything regarded as funny or appropriate might be offensive or puzzling in another. Cultural norms, values, and expectations influence ambiguous language interpretation. While direct and explicit communication is valued in certain cultures, others emphasize indirectness and use implicit clues to convey meaning. Understanding these differences in linguistic approaches and being receptive to different interpretations are essential for navigating cross-cultural communication.

Instead of being a weakness, ambiguity is a necessary component of language's variety and flexibility. Acknowledging the dynamic interaction between language forms, contextual cues, and the various interpretations that wording invites is essential in embracing ambiguity. It tests our capacity for cognitive flexibility, forcing us to make our way through a maze of contradictory interpretations and cultivating a greater understanding of the subtleties in our words. We discover the complex dance of language as we interact with the multiple nature of ambiguity, where words serve as vehicles for a constantly changing tapestry of meanings.

Context and Semantics

In the intricate tapestry of language, the interplay between context and semantics weaves a dynamic narrative, guiding the interpretation and shaping the nuanced meanings of words, phrases, and sentences.

Context acts as the silent orchestrator, providing the backdrop against which semantics unfolds its rich tapestry. This investigation explores the mutually beneficial link between context and semantics, revealing the levels of meaning that arise when words are positioned inside the ever-changing communication landscapes.

At its essence, semantics is the study of meaning in language, examining how words convey concepts and how these concepts relate to one another. However, the sense of a word extends far beyond its dictionary definition. Semantics delves into the intricate web of connotations, associations, and nuances that infuse words with life, turning them into vessels for complex ideas and emotions. The semantic field, a thematic cluster of related words, illustrates the interconnectedness of meaning within a conceptual domain. As an illustration, the semantic field "emotion" includes terms like "joy," "anger," and "sadness," each of which adds a distinct tone to the whole subject. Semantics is the art of unraveling these intricate connections, deciphering the dance of meaning within the linguistic realm.

Now introduce context, semantics' silent partner that molds and polishes meanings suggested by semantics. The crucible in which words change from abstract symbols into bearers of particular meanings in context. The rumors surrounding a given sentence or linguistic context offer essential clues for interpretation. Think about the phrase "She saw the bat." The term "bat" is still unclear without context; may it refer to a flying mammal or a piece of sporting equipment? The surrounding words and the broader discourse context guide our interpretation, disambiguating the meaning based on the situational cues provided.

Pragmatics, a branch of linguistics closely intertwined with semantics, explores the use of language in context. It recognizes that the interpretation of linguistic expressions depends not only on their literal meanings but also on the shared knowledge, social conventions, and situational context in which they are used. Grice's Cooperative Principle, a fundamental principle in pragmatics, outlines the expectations that speakers and listeners have for cooperative communication. The four maxims—Quantity, Quality, Relation, and Manner—are benchmarks for productive dialogue in a particular setting. Pragmatic considerations are essential to resolve ambiguity, make intentions clear, and ensure that meaning matches the expectations of the speaker and the listener.

Anaphora and deixis, pragmatic phenomena deeply entwined with context, illuminate the dynamic nature of reference in language. Anaphora is returning to a previous point in the speech and creating a relationship between them using the context. In the sentence "John lost his wallet; he was distraught," the pronoun "he" draws its meaning from the context established by the preceding mention of John. Conversely, deixis refers to words whose meaning depends on extralinguistic context, including the speaker's location in space or time. The word "this" in the sentence "I like this" gains specificity only when the speaker and the listener share an everyday visual or situational context. Anaphora and deixis exemplify how context plays a fundamental role in determining the referential meaning of words within a discourse.

Semantic ambiguity, a common feature of language, resolves through the contextual cues provided by situational and linguistic contexts. Although lexical terms like "bank" and "bark" may have several meanings, their intended context makes them apparent. The sentence "The dog barked at the bank" takes on a different meaning depending on whether "bark" refers to the sound a dog makes or the outer covering of a tree. The context, shaped by the surrounding words and the broader narrative, guides the listener or reader in discerning the intended meaning.

The interaction between context and semantics becomes particularly nuanced in polysemy—the phenomenon where a single word has multiple related meanings. Polysemous words derive their distinct senses from a shared underlying concept, and the disambiguation often hinges on contextual clues. Think about the term "bank" again. In the context of a river, it refers to the side of the watercourse, while in a financial setting, it denotes a financial institution. The context in which "bank" appears guides the listener or reader in selecting the relevant meaning, showcasing the dynamic nature of word interpretation within the semantic landscape.

The interaction between context and semantics is further complicated by cultural context. Different cultures may attribute varied connotations and associations to the same word, influencing how it is understood and interpreted. For instance, the term "freedom" carries different historical and cultural resonances in the context of the United States compared to China. Cultural nuances shape the semantic landscape, adding layers of meaning that extend beyond the words themselves. Cross-cultural communication demands an awareness of these cultural contexts to facilitate accurate interpretation and avoid misunderstandings.

The significance of context in semantics becomes even more apparent when examining the phenomenon of semantic shift over time. Words evolve, acquiring new meanings or shedding old ones in response to social, cultural, or technological changes. The term "gay," for example, has undergone a significant semantic shift from its original meaning of "happy" to its contemporary connotation related to sexual orientation. Changes in societal attitudes and cultural circumstances considerably impact the formation of importance, demonstrating the dynamic nature of language and its ability to adapt to the always-shifting terrain of human experience.

Ambiguity, frequently regarded as a communication difficulty, is resolved by the subtle interaction between context and semantics. Even though a sentence alone may have multiple meanings, the surrounding context is a clarifying lens that points the reader or listener toward the intended purpose. The sentence "I saw the man with the telescope" exemplifies how syntactic ambiguity dissolves within a broader context, allowing for a more precise interpretation. The context clarifies whether the speaker saw a man via a telescope or saw a man through a telescope, demonstrating the effectiveness of situational signals in linguistic disambiguation.

In conclusion, the relationship between context and semantics is an intricate dance that gives life to the meanings encoded in language. Word meaning is revealed by semantics, and the context creates the stage on which meaning is revealed. The symbiotic interplay between the two shapes the dynamic communication landscape, allowing for the fluidity, adaptability, and richness that characterize human language. As we navigate this dance of meaning, we gain a deeper appreciation for how context and semantics collaborate to convey human thought and expression complexities.

Practical Applications of Semantic Analysis

Semantic analysis, a field at the intersection of linguistics and computer science, holds the key to unlocking the meaningful insights embedded in vast troves of textual data. Beyond mere syntactic structures, semantic analysis delves into the deeper layers of meaning, discerning context, relationships, and sentiments within language. This exploration navigates the practical applications of semantic analysis, revealing its transformative impact across diverse domains, from artificial intelligence and business intelligence to customer experience and healthcare.

One of the foremost applications of semantic analysis resides in Natural Language Processing (NLP), a subfield of artificial intelligence. NLP endeavors to bridge the gap between human language and machine understanding, enabling computers to comprehend, interpret, and generate human-like text. Semantic analysis plays a pivotal role in this endeavor by going beyond the surface-level structures of language. It breaks down the text's relationships, meanings, and subtleties so that robots may understand context, deduce meanings, and react wisely. Chatbots and virtual assistants, powered by sophisticated semantic analysis algorithms, exemplify the practical manifestation of this technology, engaging in context-aware conversations and providing users with tailored responses based on the meaning extracted from their input.

Semantic analysis emerges as a potent tool for extracting actionable insights from textual data in business intelligence and data analytics. As organizations amass vast volumes of unstructured data—from customer reviews and social media posts to internal documents and emails—making sense of this information becomes a formidable challenge. Raw text is transformed into organized, understandable data using semantic analysis, revealing feelings, patterns, and trends that guide strategic decision-making. Sentiment analysis, a specific application within the semantic analysis, discerns the emotional tone conveyed in a text, helping businesses gauge customer satisfaction, brand perception, and market sentiment. The ability to extract meaning from textual data positions semantic analysis as a cornerstone in the data-driven decision-making paradigm.

In the customer experience domain, semantic analysis is a powerful ally in understanding and responding to customer needs. Customer feedback, expressed through various channels, contains valuable information that can shape product development, service improvements, and overall brand strategy. Semantic analysis dissects this feedback, identifying key themes, sentiments, and areas for improvement. Real-time semantic analysis improves customer service interactions by allowing businesses to react quickly to customer questions, issues, or feedback with a deeper level of comprehension than just keyword matching. By deciphering the nuanced meanings within customer interactions, businesses can tailor their responses, enhance customer satisfaction, and build stronger, more meaningful relationships.

Healthcare, a field inherently rich in textual data—from medical records and research papers to patient narratives—embraces semantic analysis for improved patient care, research, and knowledge discovery. Extracting meaningful information from medical texts, such as clinical notes or research articles, enables healthcare professionals and researchers to stay abreast of the latest developments, identify relevant studies, and enhance diagnostic accuracy. Semantically driven clinical decision support systems combine medical literature to give doctors evidence-based insights, leading to better informed and individualized patient treatment. The nuanced understanding of medical terminology and context afforded by semantic analysis facilitates the integration of diverse healthcare datasets, paving the way for holistic approaches to patient treatment and population health management.

Semantic analysis becomes a crucial component in the dynamic world of e-commerce, helping improve search functions and elevate the user experience. Conventional keyword-based searches frequently need to catch the subtleties of user intent. Semantic search, fueled by semantic analysis, goes beyond mere keyword matching, considering the meaning and context of user queries. This enables e-commerce platforms to deliver more relevant and accurate search results, improving product discoverability and customer satisfaction. Semantic analysis also helps with product classification and recommendation by providing a deeper understanding of the user's characteristics, features, and preferences. The result is a more intuitive and personalized shopping experience that aligns with the evolving expectations of today's online consumers.

In cybersecurity, where the volume and complexity of textual data pose significant challenges, semantic analysis emerges as a vital weapon in the arsenal against cyber threats. Analyzing logs, incident reports, and security alerts requires a nuanced understanding of the language used in these contexts. Patterns, anomalies, and potential security threats concealed inside textual data can be found via semantic analysis. By discerning the semantics of communication and identifying abnormal patterns of behavior, cybersecurity professionals can detect and respond to threats more effectively. Moreover, semantic analysis contributes to developing advanced threat intelligence systems, where extracting meaningful information from diverse sources empowers organizations to avoid emerging cyber threats.

Legal professionals grapple with vast volumes of legal texts, case law, and documents, making semantic analysis valuable in legal research and analysis. Semantic technologies facilitate the extraction of relevant legal concepts, relationships, and precedents from extensive legal databases. This expedites the legal research process and enhances the accuracy of legal insights by considering the semantic context within which legal terms and concepts are used. Semantic analysis goes beyond research to assist in contract analysis by highlighting essential words, responsibilities, and possible dangers in legal contracts. Semantic analysis tools are valuable for legal practitioners to improve productivity, optimize workflow, and obtain a deeper understanding of the law.

The advent of the Semantic Web: based on semantic technologies, this concept, supported by World Wide Web inventor Sir Tim Berners-Lee, aims to increase web content accessibility and interoperability. By annotating web content with semantic metadata, machines can better understand the meaning and relationships between different pieces of information. This enables more sophisticated search engines, tailored content suggestions, and smooth information fusion across many platforms. The Semantic Web aims to transform the web into a global knowledge base where data is linked and imbued with meaning, fostering a more connected and intelligent digital ecosystem.

In conclusion, the practical applications of semantic analysis traverse a diverse landscape, from artificial intelligence and business intelligence to customer experience, healthcare, e-commerce, cybersecurity, and legal research. As a bridge between the richness of human language and the analytical capabilities of machines, semantic analysis unlocks the power of meaningful data. Its capacity to discern context, relationships, and sentiments within textual data positions it as a transformative force, shaping industries and domains by offering more profound insights, improving decision-making processes, and enhancing user experiences. As technology advances, semantic analysis will only intensify, guiding us toward a future where the meaning within data becomes an invaluable asset for innovation and progress.

Chapter V

Pragmatics:
Beyond Syntax and Semantics

Definition and Role of Pragmatics

Pragmatics, a subfield of linguistics, serves as the lens through which we understand communication's nuanced and context-dependent nature. While syntax and semantics focus on the structure and meaning of language, pragmatics delves into how language is used in context, emphasizing the social and situational aspects that shape substance. This investigation explores the purpose and use of pragmatics, revealing the complex dynamics that direct communication and shape the pragmatic decisions we make while interacting with language.

At its core, pragmatics concerns the study of language use in context—the way speakers employ language to achieve their communicative goals within specific social and situational settings. Unlike syntax, which examines the grammatical structure of sentences, or semantics, which delves into word meanings and their relationships, pragmatics looks beyond the literal interpretation of words and sentences. It recognizes that meaning is more than just language; it's also about shared knowledge, cultural norms, and the dynamic interaction between speakers and listeners.

H.P. Grice, a philosopher, introduced implicature, one of the core ideas of pragmatics. Grice's Cooperative Principle assumes that participants strive to be cooperative and informative in communication. In this context, implicatures occur when speakers rely on the cooperation and expectations of their listeners to communicate meaning subtly. Conversational implicatures, for instance, allow speakers to share more than what is explicitly stated, drawing on the assumption that participants will infer additional information based on the context and cooperative nature of the interaction.

Pragmatics also delves into deixis, a phenomenon where the interpretation of certain words or expressions depends on the extralinguistic context, such as the spatial or temporal location of the speaker. Pronouns like "this," "that," "here," and "there" gain specificity only when the speaker and the listener share a common understanding of the referential context. Deictic expressions highlight the pragmatic sensitivity of language, where meaning is not fixed within the words themselves but emerges in the interaction between linguistic forms and situational context.

Another essential component of pragmatics is speech acts, which center on the performative role of language—the notion that utterances can execute actions in addition to delivering information. Philosopher J.L. Austin introduced the concept of speech acts, categorizing reports into illocutionary acts (the intended action behind the word) and perlocutionary acts (the effect the word has on the listener). For instance, when someone says, "I promise to be there on time," they are completing the act of making a promise rather than just stating it. The speaker's aim and the listener's understanding within the communication context determine whether or not a speech act is successful.

Politeness theory, developed by sociolinguists Erving Goffman and Penelope Brown, explores speakers' intricate strategies to mitigate potential face-threatening acts and maintain positive social interactions. Face, in this context, refers to a person's social value and sense of self-esteem in a given exchange. Politeness strategies, such as using indirect language, mitigating expressions, or employing positive politeness to show friendliness, illustrate how pragmatics intersects with social dynamics. Understanding and navigating politeness norms are integral to effective communication in diverse cultural and social contexts.

The study of deixis, implicature, speech acts, and politeness represents just a fraction of pragmatics's vast landscape. Anaphora, reference resolution, and the role of context in utterance interpretation further enrich the pragmatic toolkit. Moreover, the practical analysis extends beyond spoken language to encompass written communication, where authors make strategic choices to convey meaning and achieve rhetorical goals. Pragmatics is a field that is constantly changing to accommodate the intricate and varied aspects of human communication.

Pragmatics plays a pivotal role in uncovering the intricacies of cross-cultural communication. Cultural differences in manners of speaking, deference to authority, and indirectness all significantly influence the pragmatic decisions that speakers make. The idea of "face," which is fundamental to many Asian cultures, shapes communication dynamics by strongly emphasizing maintaining social harmony and avoiding outright conflict. In contrast, Western cultures may value individual expression and directness more. Pragmatic awareness becomes essential to navigate these cultural quirks, promote successful communication, and prevent misunderstandings.

The role of pragmatics extends beyond theoretical inquiry, finding practical applications in various domains. In education, an understanding of pragmatics informs language teaching methodologies, emphasizing the importance of contextualized language use. Pragmatic competence becomes a valuable skill for language learners, enabling them to navigate real-world communication situations with cultural sensitivity and effective language use. Additionally, in artificial intelligence, incorporating pragmatic knowledge into natural language processing systems enhances their ability to comprehend and generate contextually appropriate responses, bringing machines closer to human-like communication.

Pragmatics is practical in clinical and therapeutic settings, especially in speech and language pathology. Individuals with pragmatic language disorders may struggle with social communication, failing to grasp the implicit meanings, sarcasm, or indirect cues embedded in everyday interactions. Using pragmatics, speech-language pathologists create therapies that improve people's pragmatic ability and help them deal with social circumstances more skillfully. Building and sustaining connections, participating in group activities, and excelling in educational and professional contexts all depend on pragmatic language abilities.

The legal field also benefits from the insights provided by pragmatics, especially in the interpretation of legal texts and the analysis of witness testimony. Pragmatic analysis helps legal professionals decipher the intended meaning behind ambiguous language, understand the illocutionary force of legal statements, and navigate the nuances of courtroom communication. By acknowledging the pragmatic dimensions of legal terminology, practitioners can enhance their interpretative skills and contribute to more accurate legal analyses.

To sum up, pragmatics is a lens that helps us understand the complex dynamics of meaning in communication. Examining speech acts, implicature, deixis, politeness, and cultural variances enhances our comprehension of language use in context. Beyond theoretical inquiry, pragmatics finds practical applications in diverse fields, from education and artificial intelligence to clinical settings and the legal domain. As we navigate the complex tapestry of human interaction, pragmatics stands as a guiding force, unveiling the nuanced choices we make in our linguistic exchanges and contributing to the practical and meaningful communication that defines our social interactions.

Speech Acts and Intentions to Communicate

Language is a social activity involving numerous activities through speech, not only a means of information transmission. Speech acts, pioneered by philosopher J.L. Austin and later developed by John Searle, delve into the notion that utterances go beyond conveying meaning—they are acts with the power to perform actions, shape relationships, and influence the social reality in which they occur. This investigation explores the space of speech acts, illuminating their function in verbal exchanges and the complex dance of communicative intentions that underpins human language exchanges.

The fundamental tenet of speech act theory is that speech acts serve as both means of action and thought expression. Austin distinguished between illocutionary acts (the essential act of producing sounds and words), illocutionary acts (the speaker's intended activity in making an utterance), and perlocutionary acts (the effect of the report on the listener or recipient). The communicative goal of the speaker—what the speaker hopes to achieve with the utterance—is best captured by the illocutionary act in particular.

Speech acts come in various forms, each corresponding to a different illocutionary force. Austin distinguished five main types of illocutionary actions: directives (trying to persuade the listener to do something), expressive (expressing the speaker's emotions or attitudes), declarative (changing the external reality through the act of speaking), and assertive (committing the speaker to the truth of a proposition). Each illocutionary action reflects a different speech act function, and speakers navigate these functions based on their communicative goals and intentions.

Remember the phrase, "I promise to be there on time." In this utterance, the illocutionary force is commissive—the speaker is committing to a future course of action. The promise is in words themselves, and when spoken honestly, the speaker communicates ideas and makes a pledge that may or may not come to pass. The capacity of promises, apologies, demands, and other speech acts to alter social reality via spoken word makes them performative.

The success of a speech act depends on the alignment between the illocutionary force and the perlocutionary effect—the impact on the listener or recipient. Achieving this alignment requires shared linguistic and cultural conventions and an understanding of the contextual cues that shape interpretation. Misalignments can lead to misunderstandings, and the effectiveness of speech acts hinges on the speaker's ability to accurately gauge the listener's performance.

Indirect speech acts, a phenomenon explored by linguist H.P. Grice, add complexity to the dynamics of communicative intentions. In indirect speech acts, the speaker conveys their intended illocutionary force indirectly, relying on the listener's ability to infer the underlying communicative intent. When someone says, "It's cold in here," for instance, they express the precise truth about the temperature, but they may also indirectly ask you to close the window. The listener must recognize the indirect request through contextual cues and shared cultural norms.

Politeness strategies, often intertwined with indirect speech acts, highlight speakers' pragmatic sensitivity to their communicative interactions. Brown and Levinson's politeness theory identifies two types of politeness strategies: positive politeness, which emphasizes shared values and camaraderie, and negative politeness, which highlights the speaker's desire to minimize imposition on the listener. Politeness strategies shape the illocutionary force of utterances, allowing speakers to navigate social hierarchies, maintain face, and engage in cooperative communication.

The cultural context significantly influences the realization of speech acts and communicative intentions. Different cultures may prioritize certain speech act functions or employ distinct linguistic strategies to achieve communicative goals. Directness and indirectness, levels of formality, and expectations regarding politeness vary across cultures, contributing to the diverse tapestry of global communication. Understanding these differences and having the ability to negotiate the subtleties of communicative intentions in many cultural contexts are prerequisites for cross-cultural communication competency.

In addition to their role in everyday conversation, speech acts are crucial in legal and political discourse. Legal documents, contracts, and legislative texts include speech acts that have the authority to establish duties, rights, and legal ramifications. International accords and diplomatic ties are shaped by statements and pledges made in political discourse. Political speeches are performative, with leaders making promises, announcing plans, or giving orders. This shows how speech acts transcend the private sphere and impact larger social and political realities.

The digital age introduces new dimensions to studying speech acts and communicative intentions. Online communication platforms, social media, and digital interactions bring unique challenges and opportunities for analyzing speech acts in virtual spaces. The brevity of messages, the absence of nonverbal cues, and the speed of online interactions influence how communicative intentions are conveyed and interpreted. The study of speech acts in the digital sphere is made more complex by using hashtags, emoticons, and other digital affordances.

Understanding the dynamics of speech acts is crucial for effective communication in professional settings. A complicated interplay of speech acts occurs in business meetings, negotiations, and presentations—Assertiveness, directiveness, and commissives all influence how encounters turn out. Fostering a collaborative and productive work environment requires leaders and managers to know the communication intentions underlying words. Miscommunications can have significant consequences, highlighting the importance of pragmatic competence in the workplace.

In summary, speech acts and communicative intentions are the cornerstones of verbal communication, influencing the interactions, social contexts, and behaviors that occur when language is employed. From promises and requests to declarations and apologies, speech acts perform myriad functions in our daily interactions. The study of speech act theory offers insights into the nuanced dynamics of illocutionary forces, perlocutionary effects, indirect speech acts, and politeness strategies. As we navigate the intricate landscape of human communication, an awareness of speech acts and their communicative intentions enhances our ability to convey meaning, interpret others' intentions, and engage in effective and cooperative verbal exchanges.

Cultural and Social Influences on Pragmatics

Communication is not a one-size-fits-all endeavor; it is deeply influenced by cultural and social contexts that shape how individuals express themselves and interpret others. Through the perspective of pragmatics—the study of language use in context—we may examine the substantial effects of social and cultural factors on verbal interaction. This exploration delves into the dynamic interplay between pragmatics and culture, unraveling how diverse cultural norms, social hierarchies, and contextual cues influence the nuances of communicative exchanges.

Cultural differences significantly influence the pragmatic decisions people make in their language interactions. Different cultures may prioritize certain speech act functions, employ distinct politeness strategies, or navigate indirectness and directness in unique ways. The concept of "face," introduced by sociologist Erving Goffman and later incorporated into Brown and Levinson's politeness theory, encapsulates the social value and sense of self-esteem an individual maintains in a given interaction. Cultures may prioritize positive politeness, emphasizing camaraderie and shared values, or negative courtesy, focusing on the speaker's desire to minimize imposition on the listener. Understanding cultural variations in face-saving strategies is integral to effective cross-cultural communication.

The cultural dimension of power distance, as identified by cultural theorists Geert Hofstede and Edward T. Hall, also influences communicative dynamics. In cultures with high power distance, individuals may exhibit greater deference to authority figures and employ more formal language and gestures to show respect. In contrast, cultures with low power distance may encourage a more egalitarian and informal communication style. These cultural differences are reflected in speech acts, courteous expressions, and the general tone of communication exchanges, reflecting broader cultural attitudes about hierarchy and authority.

Expressions of politeness, a core aspect of pragmatic competence, vary across cultures, influencing how individuals initiate and respond to communicative acts. In East Asian cultures, for example, politeness often involves indirect language, implicit expressions, and a focus on maintaining harmony. Conversely, Western cultures may place a higher value on directness and explicitness in communication. These cultural preferences extend to greetings, address terms, and formulaic expressions that convey respect, friendliness, or formality based on cultural norms.

The influence of cultural context becomes particularly apparent in indirect speech acts. Certain cultures value indirection as a courteous tactic or a way to discuss delicate subjects, while others value clear and concise communication. The interpretation of indirect speech acts relies on shared cultural conventions and an understanding of contextual cues, making cross-cultural communication a delicate dance of navigating these subtle nuances.

Cultural differences also affect expectations about quiet and pauses, turn-taking, and conversational conventions. In some cultures, a delay may signify contemplation or emphasis; in others, it may be interpreted as discomfort or hesitation. The rhythm and flow of conversation, influenced by cultural norms, impact the overall dynamics of verbal interaction. Understanding the cultural context is crucial for interpreting these cues accurately and engaging in communication that aligns with cultural expectations.

Social hierarchies and societal power dynamics further shape pragmatic choices and communicative patterns. Language can be used to uphold or undermine social norms and orders of power. Using honorifics, formal address terms, or specific linguistic markers of respect reflects the societal expectations surrounding deference and authority. In workplace settings, the language used in interactions between superiors and subordinates and among peers is often influenced by hierarchical structures and professional norms.

Cultural and social influences on pragmatics extend to nonverbal communication, including gestures, body language, and facial expressions. Different cultures ascribe meanings to nonverbal cues, and individuals from diverse cultural backgrounds may interpret gestures differently. The significance of eye contact, the appropriateness of physical proximity, and the use of hand gestures can all be influenced by cultural norms. Misinterpretations of nonverbal cues can lead to misunderstandings and highlight the importance of cultural awareness in navigating nonverbal aspects of communication.

The intersection of pragmatics and culture becomes particularly salient in the era of globalization and multiculturalism. Individuals from different cultural backgrounds interact in diverse settings, bringing a mosaic of communicative styles and expectations. Understanding cultural differences in pragmatics, being open to adjusting to other communication standards, and negotiating the intricacies of language and cultural variety are all necessary for effective cross-cultural communication.

Social identity and group membership also play a role in shaping communicative patterns. Subcultures can form specific, pragmatic norms that represent the distinctive qualities of the group. Shared values, beliefs, and practices characterize subcultures. For example, youth subcultures, professional communities, or online communities may exhibit specific linguistic features and communication styles that align with their shared identity.

The role of pragmatics in intercultural communication is not solely about recognizing differences; it also involves building bridges and fostering mutual understanding. Effective cross-cultural communication requires intercultural competency, more than just recognizing cultural differences. It also requires actively participating in courteous and flexible conversation. Individuals who possess intercultural competence can navigate diverse cultural contexts with sensitivity, recognizing the influence of cultural and social factors on pragmatics and adjusting their communicative strategies accordingly.

In conclusion, cultural and social influences on pragmatics shape the intricate tapestry of verbal communication. From speech act functions and politeness strategies to nonverbal cues and conversational norms, the interplay between pragmatics and culture defines the nuances of communicative exchanges. Comprehending these factors is imperative for proficient cross-cultural correspondence, cultivating intercultural proficiency, and maneuvering through the intricacies of a worldwide and diverse society. As we engage in conversations that transcend cultural boundaries, an awareness of pragmatics's cultural and social dimensions enriches our ability to communicate meaningfully and build connections across diverse linguistic landscapes.

Improving Interaction Through Realistic Proficiency

Communication is a dynamic interplay of words, gestures, and context—a nuanced dance where meaning is conveyed through language and shaped by the subtleties of social interaction. This exploration delves into the multifaceted dimensions of pragmatic competence, uncovering its significance in navigating diverse communicative situations, fostering positive social interactions, and enhancing the overall quality of human connection.

At its essence, pragmatic competence involves more than linguistic proficiency; it encompasses understanding the social and cultural nuances that influence how language is used and interpreted. Pragmatics studies how speakers use language to accomplish their communication objectives in particular social and environmental contexts. From speech acts and politeness strategies to indirect speech and contextual cues, pragmatic competence navigates the complex terrain of verbal interaction, requiring individuals to decipher the unspoken rules that govern communication.

One fundamental aspect of pragmatic competence is recognizing and appropriately using speech acts—the performative functions of language beyond the mere transmission of information. In addition to conveying meaning, words can be used to carry out actions. Whether making promises, giving commands, expressing apologies, or engaging in declarations, pragmatic competence empowers individuals to deploy speech acts effectively based on the communicative context and their intended impact. Being proficient in speech acts is like having a multipurpose toolkit that lets people use words to create the social reality they want

Politeness strategies, another cornerstone of pragmatic competence, come into play as individuals navigate social hierarchies, power dynamics, and relational nuances in communication. The politeness theory developed by Brown and Levinson describes how people use language to protect their reputations, fend off dangers, and sustain cordial social relationships. When employing positive politeness, emphasizing shared values and camaraderie, or negative refinement, minimizing imposition on the listener is a skill embedded in pragmatic competence. In addition to facilitating effective communication, politeness techniques show awareness of the social and cultural forces at work.

Indirect speaking is a skill that enhances communication and is deeply ingrained in pragmatic competence. Indirectness allows speakers to convey meaning subtly, relying on the listener's ability to infer the intended message. Navigating indirect speech acts requires a heightened pragmatic awareness where the illocutionary force differs from the literal meaning. This skill becomes particularly crucial when cultural norms favor indirectness as a form of politeness or where the explicit expression of specific ideas may be culturally discouraged.

A key component of pragmatic competence, contextual cues offer the framework for successful communication. The capacity to recognize and react to contextual cues, be they verbal, nonverbal, or situational, allows people to modify their language use in real time. This responsiveness to context extends to understanding social roles, power dynamics, and the overarching cultural norms that shape communication. In addition to being proficient language users, pragmatic competence encourages people to be contextually aware communicators who can quickly move through various settings.

The ramifications of pragmatic competence are not limited to personal relations; they also have significant effects in professional contexts. Pragmatic competence contributes to effective collaboration, team dynamics, and leadership communication in the workplace. The mastery of speech acts allows leaders to inspire and motivate, while awareness of politeness strategies fosters a positive and inclusive organizational culture. Navigating indirect speech and contextual cues becomes instrumental in successful negotiations, resolving conflicts, and building strong interpersonal relationships within the professional sphere.

In educational contexts, pragmatic competence is critical to language learning and development. In addition to picking up language patterns, language learners also absorb the social and cultural conventions that dictate communication. Pragmatic awareness enables individuals to engage in appropriate conversational exchanges, participate in classroom discussions, and express themselves effectively within social and cultural expectations. As language education evolves, a focus on pragmatic competence becomes imperative to prepare learners for real-world communication scenarios.

The digital age introduces new dimensions to pragmatic competence, especially online communication. In virtual environments, people depend more on linguistic signals and contextual awareness because there are fewer nonverbal signs and no immediate face-to-face connection. Navigating digital politeness, interpreting the nuances of online speech acts, and understanding the cultural diversity inherent in virtual interactions become integral to effective communication in the digital realm.

In a world where connections are growing, cultural competence—intimately related to pragmatic competence—is crucial. Communication across cultural boundaries necessitates knowledge of various linguistic conventions, cultural norms, and communicative styles. By serving as a bridge, pragmatic competence promotes interactions that cut over linguistic and cultural divides and aids in cross-cultural understanding. As global collaboration becomes the norm rather than the exception, individuals who possess pragmatic competence contribute to creating inclusive and culturally sensitive communication spaces.

In therapeutic and clinical settings, pragmatic competence takes on a therapeutic role. Speech-language pathologists, counselors, and mental health professionals leverage pragmatic competence to navigate the complexities of verbal interaction with clients. Professionals can comprehend clients' communicative goals, manage social communication difficulties, and provide a helpful therapy environment by thoroughly understanding the pragmatic components of language. Practical therapies are tools for improving social skills, controlling social anxiety, and encouraging productive communication techniques.

In conclusion, enhancing communication through pragmatic competence is a journey of contextual mastery—an ongoing process of understanding, adapting, and utilizing language to align with social and cultural expectations. From speech acts and politeness strategies to the navigation of indirect speech and contextual cues, pragmatic competence empowers individuals to communicate effectively across diverse settings. It is important in interpersonal relationships and the more general domains of education, professional cooperation, intercultural dialogue, and therapeutic practice. In a world that is changing quickly, pragmatic competence is a valuable tool for people as they work to become skilled communicators. It shows the path toward relevant and influential conversations.

Enhancing Communication Through Pragmatic Competence

Communication is a dynamic interplay of words, gestures, and context—a nuanced dance where meaning is conveyed through language and shaped by the subtleties of social interaction. One of the most critical aspects of learning the craft of effective communication is developing pragmatic competency, or the ability to speak and write clearly in a particular context. Pragmatic competence, the ability to manipulate language appropriately in a given context, emerges as a critical facet in mastering the art of effective communication. This exploration delves into the multifaceted dimensions of pragmatic competence, uncovering its significance in navigating diverse communicative situations, fostering positive social interactions, and enhancing the overall quality of human connection.

At its essence, pragmatic competence involves more than linguistic proficiency; it encompasses understanding the social and cultural nuances that influence how language is used and interpreted. Pragmatics studies how speakers use language to accomplish their communication objectives in particular social and environmental contexts. From speech acts and politeness strategies to indirect speech and contextual cues, pragmatic competence navigates the complex terrain of verbal interaction, requiring individuals to decipher the unspoken rules that govern communication.

One fundamental aspect of pragmatic competence is recognizing and appropriately using speech acts—the performative functions of language beyond the mere transmission of information. In addition to conveying meaning, words can be used to carry out actions.

Whether making promises, giving commands, expressing apologies, or engaging in declarations, pragmatic competence empowers individuals to deploy speech acts effectively based on the communicative context and their intended impact. Being proficient in speech acts is like having a multipurpose toolkit that lets people use words to create the social reality they want.

Politeness strategies, another cornerstone of pragmatic competence, come into play as individuals navigate social hierarchies, power dynamics, and relational nuances in communication. The politeness theory developed by Brown and Levinson describes how people use language to protect their reputations, fend off dangers, and sustain cordial social relationships. When employing positive politeness, emphasizing shared values and camaraderie, or negative refinement, minimizing imposition on the listener is a skill embedded in pragmatic competence. In addition to facilitating effective communication, politeness techniques show awareness of the social and cultural forces at work.

Indirect speaking is a skill that enhances communication and is deeply ingrained in pragmatic competence. Indirectness allows speakers to convey meaning subtly, relying on the listener's ability to infer the intended message. Navigating indirect speech acts requires a heightened pragmatic awareness where the illocutionary force differs from the literal meaning. This skill becomes particularly crucial when cultural norms favor indirectness as a form of politeness or where the explicit expression of specific ideas may be culturally discouraged.

A key component of pragmatic competence, contextual cues offer the framework for successful communication. The capacity to recognize and react to contextual cues, be they verbal, nonverbal, or situational, allows people to modify their language use in real time. This responsiveness to context extends to understanding social roles, power dynamics, and the overarching cultural norms that shape communication. In addition to being proficient language users, pragmatic competence encourages people to be contextually aware communicators who can quickly move through various settings.

The ramifications of pragmatic competence are not limited to personal relations; they also have significant effects in professional contexts. Pragmatic competence contributes to effective collaboration, team dynamics, and leadership communication in the workplace. Mastering speech acts allows leaders to inspire and motivate, while awareness of politeness strategies fosters a positive and inclusive organizational culture. Navigating indirect speech and contextual cues becomes instrumental in successful negotiations, resolving conflicts, and building strong interpersonal relationships within the professional sphere.

In educational contexts, pragmatic competence is critical to language learning and development. In addition to picking up language patterns, language learners also absorb the social and cultural conventions that dictate communication. Pragmatic awareness enables individuals to engage in appropriate conversational exchanges, participate in classroom discussions, and express themselves effectively within social and cultural expectations. As language education evolves, a focus on pragmatic competence becomes imperative to prepare learners for real-world communication scenarios.

The digital age introduces new dimensions to pragmatic competence, especially online communication. In virtual environments, people depend more on linguistic signals and contextual awareness because there are fewer nonverbal signs and no immediate face-to-face connection. Navigating digital politeness, interpreting the nuances of online speech acts, and understanding the cultural diversity inherent in virtual interactions become integral to effective communication in the digital realm.

In a world where connections are growing, cultural competence—intimately related to pragmatic competence—is crucial. Communication across cultural boundaries necessitates knowledge of various linguistic conventions, cultural norms, and communicative styles. By serving as a bridge, pragmatic competence promotes interactions that cut over linguistic and cultural divides and aids in cross-cultural understanding. As global collaboration becomes the norm rather than the exception, individuals who possess pragmatic competence contribute to creating inclusive and culturally sensitive communication spaces.

In therapeutic and clinical settings, pragmatic competence takes on a therapeutic role. Speech-language pathologists, counselors, and mental health professionals leverage pragmatic competence to navigate the complexities of verbal interaction with clients. Professionals can comprehend clients' communicative goals, manage social communication difficulties, and provide a helpful therapy environment by thoroughly understanding the pragmatic components of language. Practical therapies are tools for improving social skills, controlling social anxiety, and encouraging productive communication techniques.

In conclusion, enhancing communication through pragmatic competence is a journey of contextual mastery—an ongoing process of understanding, adapting, and utilizing language to align with social and cultural expectations. From speech acts and politeness strategies to the navigation of indirect speech and contextual cues, pragmatic competence empowers individuals to communicate effectively across diverse settings. It is important in interpersonal relationships and the more general domains of education, professional cooperation, intercultural dialogue, and therapeutic practice. In a world that is changing quickly, pragmatic competence is a valuable tool for people as they work to become skilled communicators. It shows the path toward relevant and influential conversations.

Chapter VI

Cognitive Linguistics

Language and Thought

The relationship between language and thought is a subject of profound inquiry that has captivated scholars, philosophers, and linguists throughout history. At the heart of this exploration is the fundamental question: to what extent does language shape our thoughts, and conversely, how do our thoughts influence how we use language? This intricate interplay between language and thought forms a symbiotic relationship, shaping cognition, perception, and our understanding of the world. This section delves into the multifaceted dimensions of this symbiosis, examining how language serves as a vehicle for thought, influences our conceptualizations of reality, and acts as a dynamic force in shaping the human mind.

Language, a complex system of symbols and rules, is a medium through which thoughts are externalized and shared. Linguist Benjamin Lee Whorf proposed the linguistic relativity hypothesis, suggesting that a language's structure may affect how speakers understand and interpret the world. The hypothesis posits that different languages provide distinct cognitive frameworks, shaping how individuals express their thoughts and how they conceptualize and categorize their experiences. The theory of linguistic determinism—which holds that language controls or limits thought—was inspired by Whorf's ideas. While strong linguistic determinism has faced criticism, scholars acknowledge a more nuanced version known as linguistic relativity, highlighting the influence of language on cognitive processes.

One prominent area where linguistic relativity is apparent is in the perception of color. Different languages categorize and label colors in diverse ways, and studies have shown that speakers of languages with distinct color categories perceive and discriminate colors differently. Languages that lack or have particular color terminology can affect a person's ability to distinguish between different shades of a color. This phenomenon suggests that the linguistic distinctions embedded in color terms influence individuals' perceptual boundaries within the color spectrum, providing insights into the intricate connection between language and cognitive processes.

Beyond color perception, language shapes the way individuals conceptualize and express abstract concepts. The presence or absence of specific words or lexical categories in a language can influence the salience and accessibility of particular ideas. For instance, the Sapir-Whorf hypothesis suggests that languages with more elaborate tense systems may lead speakers to be more attuned to the temporal dimension of events. In languages where time is expressed with greater granularity, speakers may develop a heightened sensitivity to temporal nuances, influencing how they structure and recall material information. This demonstrates how language can be a cognitive scaffold, affecting how people organize and conceptualize their experiences.

While linguistic relativity suggests language influences thought, the relationship is bidirectional—thought also shapes language. The creativity and flexibility of human thought find expression in the rich tapestry of linguistic diversity. Thought processes, including abstract reasoning, problem-solving, and emotional experiences, are externalized through language. Sentences, metaphors, and the expression of complicated ideas depend on the cognitive abilities that thought contributes to language. As individuals grapple with new concepts or navigate novel experiences, language becomes the medium through which thought is articulated and shared, facilitating individual and collective sense-making.

The relationship between language and thought becomes particularly evident in bilingual or multilingual individuals. The cognitive flexibility required to navigate multiple languages provides unique insights into the dynamic interplay between linguistic and mental processes. Bilingual speakers often switch between languages based on context, demonstrating an ability to adapt their linguistic expression to the communicative demands of the moment. Studies indicate that bilingualism may impact executive control, working memory, and metalinguistic awareness, among other cognitive processes. The mental demands of managing and switching between languages contribute to enhanced cognitive flexibility, showcasing the reciprocal influence between language proficiency and cognitive abilities.

The role of language in shaping thought extends beyond the individual to societal and cultural dimensions. The words and concepts embedded in a language reflect a community's values, beliefs, and cultural nuances. Linguistic expressions capture cultural norms and offer insight into a society's collective consciousness. Cultures may prioritize certain concepts or construct unique lexical categories based on their needs and worldviews. Thus, The linguistic landscape reflects cultural priorities, influencing how individuals within a community conceptualize their social reality.

As a linguistic device, metaphor exemplifies the close relationship between mind and language. Metaphors extend beyond mere linguistic embellishments; they provide a cognitive framework through which abstract concepts are understood in terms of more concrete, embodied experiences. The conceptual metaphor theory, proposed by George Lakoff and Mark Johnson, suggests that metaphor is not confined to language but is ingrained in thought. Metaphors help us make sense of the world by relating abstract concepts to more relatable and tangible ones. For example, the metaphor of time as money ("saving time," "spending time") links the abstract concept of time to the more concrete realm of financial transactions, influencing people's thoughts and conceptualization of time.

The influence of language on thought becomes especially evident in the domain of linguistic relativity as applied to spatial concepts. Languages use various spatial frameworks, affecting how speakers see and move through space. In languages that use absolute spatial terms like "north," "south," "east," and "west," speakers develop an orientation rooted in cardinal directions. In contrast, languages that use relative spatial terms like "left," "right," "in front of," and "behind" foster a frame of reference based on the speaker's perspective. This linguistic diversity in spatial expression implies that language actively changes people's thoughts and perceptions of spatial relationships in addition to reflecting them.

While the relationship between language and thought is robust, it is essential to recognize the limits of linguistic determinism. Human cognition is remarkably flexible, and individuals can transcend the constraints of their native language to engage in abstract and creative thought. The universality of specific cognitive processes suggests that shared cognitive foundations underlie human thought, irrespective of linguistic differences. Language may shape the nuances and expressions of view, but the human mind, with its innate capacity for abstraction and symbolism, transcends the linguistic boundaries that frame its expression.

In conclusion, the symbiotic relationship between language and thought is a dynamic interplay that shapes cognition, perception, and human understanding of the world. Linguistic relativity, evident in color perception, spatial concepts, and abstract reasoning, highlights the influence of language on cognitive processes. Language serves as a vehicle for cognition, demonstrating the reciprocal nature of this relationship. Bilingualism, metaphor, and cultural influences contribute to our growing comprehension of the complex relationship between language and mind. Thoughts can be externalized and shared through language. Still, given the flexibility of the human brain, it is possible that thought itself, in its creative and abstract forms, exists outside of language. The exploration of speech and thought opens a window into the complexities of human cognition, offering insights into how the mind navigates the intricate dance between words and ideas.

Conceptual Metaphors and Frames

The intricate dance between language and thought unfolds in conceptual metaphors and frames—a dynamic interplay that shapes how we perceive, understand, and navigate the world. Conceptual metaphors are cognitive tools that allow us to comprehend abstract concepts by mapping them onto more concrete sensorimotor experiences. Conversely, frames are mental constructs that mold our perception of specific areas or situations. Together, these cognitive phenomena offer a window into the rich tapestry of human cognition, revealing how metaphorical expressions and mental frameworks permeate our daily lives, influencing our perceptions, beliefs, and interactions.

The fundamental tenet of conceptual metaphors is that abstract ideas are profoundly embedded in our lived experiences rather than outside the actual world. This perspective, central to the conceptual metaphor theory introduced by George Lakoff and Mark Johnson, posits that metaphors are not mere linguistic embellishments but fundamental to thought. For example, the metaphor "Time is Money" goes beyond language; it molds our perception of time by connecting it to the tangible world of business dealings. The mapping makes understanding and communication more accessible by metaphorically clicking the abstract idea of time to more relatable and authentic experiences.

Conceptual metaphors are mental shortcuts that help us understand complicated ideas through language and intellect. For example, the metaphor "Ideas are Food" encapsulates the idea that just as we consume food for sustenance, we engage with ideas to nourish our minds. This metaphorical mapping draws on our embodied experiences with food—something essential—to convey the significance of ideas in intellectual and creative endeavors. Metaphors of this kind improve comprehension and influence our attitudes and actions about abstract ideas.

When it comes to emotions, conceptual analogies have a particularly noticeable impact. Inherently abstract and subjective, feelings are often understood through metaphorical expressions that draw on concrete, bodily experiences. The metaphor "Love is a Journey," for instance, encapsulates the idea that romantic relationships involve progress, milestones, and shared experiences, mapping the abstract concept of love onto the concrete domain of a journey. This metaphorical framing not only aids in expressing and understanding emotions but also contributes to the cultural and social construction of emotional experiences.

Lakoff and Johnson's conceptual metaphor theory states that metaphors are components of larger cognitive frameworks called frames rather than being separate occurrences. Frames structure our understanding of specific domains, organizing knowledge, beliefs, and expectations into coherent mental structures. For instance, the idea that "Argument is War" influences how we view arguments and conversations. In this frame, we use expressions like "attack," "defend," and "counterargument" to describe verbal exchanges, drawing on the metaphorical mapping of argument onto the more familiar and structured domain of war.

Frames are more than just a single metaphor; they are complete conceptual systems that organize how we perceive and comprehend various facets of existence. The structure "Time as Money," for instance, involves the metaphorical mapping of time onto money and includes a broader conceptual system that frames time management as budgeting, wasting time as squandering resources, and being efficient as maximizing productivity. These frames embed deeply into our cognitive processes, reshaping our views, directing our actions, and impacting our judgment across various disciplines.

Cognitive linguists argue that the influence of conceptual metaphors and frames is not confined to abstract or intellectual domains; they permeate everyday language and shape our mundane experiences. Expressions like "prices are rising" or "spirits lifted," for example, illustrate the metaphor "More is Up," where the metaphorical mapping of quantity into verticality affects our perception of abundance and positivity. Similarly, the "Life is a Journey" frame structures our narrative understanding of life, shaping how we interpret events, plan for the future, and make sense of our trajectories.

The universality of certain metaphors and frames across languages and cultures underscores their deep cognitive roots. While specific linguistic expressions may vary, the underlying metaphorical mappings and structures often exhibit remarkable cross-cultural consistency. For example, the metaphor "Up is Good, Down is Bad" is reflected in expressions like "morale is high" or "spirits lifted" across diverse linguistic and cultural contexts. This universality suggests that specific metaphorical mappings and frames are not arbitrary but are grounded in shared human experiences and embodied cognition.

Conceptual metaphors and frames significantly impact how topics are presented, discussed, and understood in social and political discourse. In his work on framing in politics, Lakoff argues that framing is not neutral but carries implicit values, perspectives, and worldviews. Political arguments frequently center on opposing frames that affect public perception of issues and decisions. For instance, the structure "Tax Relief" conveys a particular perspective on taxation, framing it as a burden that needs to be alleviated. Opposing frames, like "Investing in Public Services," present different viewpoints and highlight the beneficial contribution of taxes to the funding of necessary services.

The study of conceptual metaphors and frames also intersects with the fields of cognitive science, psychology, and neuroscience. The study of cognitive science examines how metaphors and frames shape mental models and thought processes. Psychological research delves into the role of metaphors in shaping attitudes, biases, and decision-making. Neuroscientific studies investigate the neural correlates of metaphor processing, illuminating the brain processes that underlie the comprehension and interpretation of metaphorical expressions.

The dynamic nature of metaphorical thinking is further exemplified by conceptual blending, a cognitive process where different conceptual domains are merged to create novel and creative insights. Through conceptual blending, people can create new meanings and ideas by combining knowledge from several sources. The ability to engage in conceptual blending underlines the flexibility and creativity inherent in symbolic thought, providing a cognitive basis for human innovation, problem-solving, and artistic expression.

While the pervasive influence of conceptual metaphors and frames on language and thought is evident, it is essential to recognize that these cognitive phenomena are not fixed or deterministic. People can question preexisting frameworks, use symbolic thinking, and develop original extended formulations. Metaphors and frames are tools humans use to navigate the complexity of their experiences, communicate effectively, and construct meaning. As linguistic beings, we are not bound by the metaphors and frames we inherit; instead, we actively shape and reshape the cognitive landscape through language and thought.

In conclusion, conceptual metaphors and frames are integral to human cognition, influencing how we perceive, conceptualize, and communicate about the world. These cognitive processes offer a window into the complex interactions between language and mind, from controlling how we interpret abstract notions to organizing entire fields of knowledge. Metaphors and frames are not passive reflections of thought; they are dynamic tools that facilitate meaning-making, foster creativity, and contribute to the rich tapestry of human expression. As we unravel the cognitive intricacies of conceptual metaphors and frames, we gain insights into how language and thought intertwine to shape our collective and individual experiences.

Embodied Cognition in Language

Embodied cognition is a paradigm that has arisen as a transformative lens to grasp the complex relationship between the mind, body, and language. It challenges traditional ideas of cognition as a disembodied activity. According to this viewpoint, emotions, the body's interaction with the environment, and sensory experiences are intricately linked to cognitive processes. Embodied cognition provides a fresh framework for investigating how language experiences form and are influenced by the body in the context of language. This paper explores the basic ideas of embodied cognition, looks at how it applies to language, and shows how language and the body interact dynamically in ways that go beyond conventional cognitive limits.

The core tenet of embodied cognition is that cognitive functions are dispersed throughout the body rather than restricted to the brain. As an essential component of understanding, language is not only processed in the impersonal space of mental images but is intricately linked to physical events. The way we gesture, the sensorimotor activity involved in producing speech, and the neuronal overlap between language processing and motor areas in the brain are all examples of how language is embodied. For instance, gesture is an essential component of language that helps convey meaning; it is not just a way to enhance speech. Studies have demonstrated the close coordination between lecture and movements, with the body lending linguistic expressions further levels of emphasis and significance.

Speech production involves sensorimotor experiences that are part of the embodied nature of language. In addition to using language processes, speaking activates the motor systems responsible for sound articulation. The complex synchronization of the tongue, lips, and vocal cords during speech production is influenced by sensory feedback, which modifies the way language is processed. The relationship between language and the motor system casts doubt on the idea that language is only an abstract, symbolic system, highlighting the physical and dynamic engagement of the body as its source.

Strong evidence from neuroscientific studies suggests language is embodied in the brain. The mirror neuron system overlaps language processing and motor areas and highlights the neurological links between language and motor activities. Mirror neurons are triggered when someone performs a particular action and when they see someone else performing the same action. They were first found in the brain of a macaque monkey. Language-wise, the mirror neuron system is involved in generating and understanding action verbs, indicating that language and motor activities share a common neural substrate. The assumption that language is intricately interwoven with the body's sensorimotor systems is reinforced by this neurological interweaving, which casts doubt on the conventional modular theory of the brain.

Embodied cognition also clarifies how emotion and perception influence language experiences. The meaning we give words and expressions depends on how our senses interact with the world and how we experience it. According to a study, people's perceptions of warmth and coldness, for instance, can affect their assessments of social relationships. People tend to associate words associated with heat with pleasant social encounters. Emotional states can also influence how language is processed, affecting how we understand and react to speech. The idea of a merely symbolic and disembodied cognitive process is questioned by the interaction of emotion, perception, and language, highlighting the embodied character of linguistic meaning.

The theory of linguistic affordances, which holds that specific linguistic terms enable particular activities or elicit distinct bodily reactions, illustrates how language is embodied. For example, hearing an instruction such as "Open the door" allows one to act like physically opening a door and conveying a symbolic meaning. Linguistic affordances show how linguistic meaning and embodied experiences are intertwined by linking language to possible bodily acts. This viewpoint emphasizes the intrinsic connection between linguistic representations and the possibility of physical participation, challenging conventional theories that divide language from action.

According to George Lakoff and Mark Johnson, conceptual metaphor is likewise a part of embodied cognition in language. By projecting abstract ideas onto more tangible, embodied experiences, conceptual metaphors enable us to see the embodied foundations of our conceptual knowledge. For instance, the metaphor "Love is a Journey" illustrates the dynamic and multifaceted character of love relationships by drawing on the embodied experience of a voyage. By allowing us to perceive and communicate abstract ideas through the prism of physical experiences, metaphorical mapping emphasizes how incorporated our mental systems are.

The study of embodied cognition has applications in education and language acquisition. By recognizing that language is displayed, teachers can create instructional strategies that use the body's capacity for learning. Utilizing the embodied resources that support meaning-making, incorporating gestures, physical movement, and interactive experiences into language training might improve language acquisition. Embodying language through movement has been found to enhance language competency overall, pronunciation, and vocabulary retention. This method is consistent with the notion that learning a language involves more than memorizing abstract principles; it also entails taking on the linguistic conventions and cultural quirks inherent in the language.

Signed languages are also types of linguistic embodiment, in addition to spoken and written forms. Sign language uses manual gestures, facial emotions, and body movements to involve the body in language expression. Examples of these languages are American Sign Language (ASL) and British Sign Language (BSL). The idea that language is only connected to speech is challenged by the embodied character of signed languages, highlighting the variety of embodied linguistic practices. Studies on signed languages offer significant perspectives on the applicability of specific embodied principles in various language manifestation modalities.

Although embodied cognition provides an insightful framework for comprehending the relationship between language and the body, it is essential to recognize its complex interplay with other cognitive processes. The significance of symbolic representation, abstract reasoning, and the influence of social and cultural variables on language formation are all acknowledged by embodied cognition. Instead, it draws attention to how dynamic and interwoven cognitive processes are, emphasizing how language and the body are mutually influencing.

Applications of Cognitive Linguistics in Everyday Life

Cognitive linguistics, a field investigating the relationship between language and cognition, extends beyond theoretical exploration to offer practical insights that resonate in everyday life. Rooted in the idea that language is intricately connected to thought and experience, cognitive linguistics unveils the cognitive mechanisms that underlie language use. This essay explores the applications of cognitive linguistics in real-world contexts, shedding light on how the principles and findings from this field contribute to our understanding of communication, learning, problem-solving, and the broader dynamics of human interaction.

A prominent use of cognitive linguistics is communication, specifically in comprehending and articulating complex concepts. The concept of conceptual metaphor, pioneered by George Lakoff and Mark Johnson, highlights the role of metaphorical expressions in shaping our understanding of abstract concepts. For example, the metaphor "Time is Money" frames our idea of time as a valuable resource that may be used or conserved. Understanding these symbolic correspondences improves communication by illuminating people's underlying conceptions of a discussion. This awareness becomes particularly crucial in diverse and cross-cultural communication, where variations in conceptual metaphors can impact mutual understanding.

The study of conceptual metaphors is helpful in industries like marketing and advertising. Advertisers leverage metaphorical expressions to create vivid mental images and evoke specific emotions associated with their products or services. By tapping into conceptual metaphors that resonate with consumers' experiences and desires, advertisers can craft messages that go beyond the literal features of a product, creating a more engaging and memorable impact. An automobile commercial, for instance that presents a car as a "partner in adventure" uses the allegory linking camaraderie and life's journey.

Cognitive linguistics offers valuable insights into language learning and pedagogy, influencing the way educators approach language instruction. The embodied nature of language, as emphasized in cognitive linguistics, underscores the importance of incorporating physical movement and experiential learning in language classrooms. According to studies, assimilation of language through gestures and interactive activities improves vocabulary retention, comprehension, and language competency overall. This approach aligns with the idea that language is not just a set of abstract rules to be memorized but a dynamic system deeply intertwined with bodily experiences.

One popular technique in cognitive linguistics is metaphor analysis, which helps understand how people create and communicate their experiences. Metaphorical expressions are significant in personal narratives, influencing how people structure and tell their stories. Psychologists and counselors gain insights into individuals' cognitive and emotional processes by analyzing the metaphors embedded in personal narratives. This method makes it easier to comprehend how people interpret their experiences and manage the complexity of their inner selves.

Cognitive linguistics also plays a role in legal discourse and argumentation. Using metaphors in legal language influences how legal concepts are understood and interpreted. Analyzing the metaphors employed in legal texts provides a window into the implicit assumptions and perspectives that underlie legal reasoning. For instance, the metaphor "Crime is a Disease" may shape policies and interventions prioritizing rehabilitation over punitive measures. This awareness of metaphorical framing in legal discourse contributes to a more nuanced understanding of the societal values and ethical considerations embedded in legal language.

In problem-solving and decision-making situations, cognitive linguistics provides an understanding of how people perceive and handle complicated problems. A phenomenon studied in cognitive linguistics called the framing effect emphasizes how the presentation or framing of a topic affects the decisions made. The options structure is sensitive for decision-makers, who frequently choose differently even when presented with the same information. Understanding the role of language in framing can enhance decision-making processes by promoting awareness of how linguistic nuances may bias or influence choices.

The application of cognitive linguistics can enhance public discourse and the execution of public policy. The way policies and messages are framed can impact public perception and response. By aligning communication strategies with the target audience's cognitive processes and conceptual structures, policymakers can enhance the effectiveness of public campaigns. For example, a health campaign framed around the metaphor "Healthy Living is a Journey" may resonate more effectively with the public, emphasizing the gradual and ongoing nature of adopting healthy habits.

In artificial intelligence and human-computer interaction, cognitive linguistics informs the design of natural language processing systems. Developing more intuitive and user-friendly interfaces is made more accessible by understanding the embodied character of language. Incorporating metaphor recognition algorithms, for instance, allows artificial intelligence systems to comprehend user input better and generate responses that align with the intended meanings. This application enhances the user experience by enabling more natural and contextually appropriate interactions between humans and machines.

Cognitive linguistics contributes to psycholinguistics by unraveling the cognitive processes underlying language comprehension and production. Based on the ideas of cognitive linguistics, language processing research explores how people create mental models of language input. The findings of this study have implications for creating successful language interventions for people who struggle with language impairments. By understanding the cognitive mechanisms involved in language processing, clinicians and speech-language pathologists can tailor interventions that address specific cognitive and linguistic challenges.

Chapter VII

Evolution of Language

Theories on the Origin of Language

The origin of language has long been a subject of fascination, debate, and speculation among scholars, linguists, and philosophers. As one of the defining features of human cognition and social interaction, language's evolutionary emergence remains an enigma, with various theories attempting to unravel the complex tapestry of factors that gave rise to this uniquely human capacity. This section explores some prominent ideas on the origin of language, delving into the intellectual journey that has sought to understand how humans first began to communicate through the intricate medium of language.

One prominent theory that has captured the imagination of scholars is the Bow-Wow theory, which suggests that language originated as an imitation of natural sounds. According to this hypothesis, early humans sought to replicate the sounds of the environment, such as the howling of wolves or the babbling of brooks. This imitation of natural sounds, akin to onomatopoeia, eventually evolved into a more sophisticated vocal communication system. While the Bow-Wow theory provides a straightforward and intuitive explanation, critics argue that it oversimplifies the complexity of language and its symbolic nature. Mere imitation of sounds, they contend, needs to explain the rich and abstract linguistic expressions that characterize human communication.

In contrast, the Ding-Dong theory proposes that language originated from the rhythmic and melodic sounds produced in communal activities such as ceremonial dances or group work. The theory suggests that early humans developed a rhythmic and flowing form of communication that evolved into more complex linguistic structures. This idea resonates with the notion that music and language share common cognitive and neural resources. Though the Ding-Dong theory recognizes the importance of social interactions, it does not address how rhythmic communication gives way to the syntactic and semantic complexity that is a part of language.

The Pooh-Pooh theory, also known as the gesture-first theory, posits that language began as a system of gestures and later evolved into spoken language. Advocates of this theory argue that gestures served as the primary mode of communication among early humans, with vocalizations gradually accompanying and eventually overshadowing gestural communication. The Pooh-Pooh theory aligns with the idea that language and gesture share a common cognitive and neural foundation, as evidenced by the close relationship between manual gestures and specific aspects of language processing in the brain. However, this theory raises questions about the factors that led to the transition from a predominantly gestural to a vocal mode of communication.

The Yo-He-Ho theory, or the singing-first theory, posits that language originated from rhythmic and melodic vocalizations during collective activities like communal labor. Advocates of this theory argue that the coordinated vocalizations during group activities served as a precursor to language, gradually acquiring syntactic and semantic complexity over time. The Yo-He-Ho theory aligns with the social context of language emergence, emphasizing the role of collective endeavors in shaping communication. However, it cannot explain the precise mechanisms by which rhythmic vocalizations evolved into the various linguistic structures found in human languages.

The La-la theory, or the musical protolanguage hypothesis, suggests that language originated from musical expressions that gradually acquired communicative functions. This idea emphasizes how language communication development is based on music's expressive and emotional qualities. Proponents contend that music's melodic and rhythmic elements served as a framework for developing increasingly intricate verbal systems. The La-la hypothesis clarifies the complex connection between language and music. Still, it also raises questions about the exact processes that led from musical expressions to language's syntactic and semantic complexity.

A more recent theory, the Ta-ta theory, emphasizes the role of tongue movements and manual gestures in the origin of language. Advocates propose that complex tongue movements, accompanied by manual gestures, formed the basis for early communicative exchanges. Over time, these tongue movements and gestures became more conventionalized, giving rise to the diverse phonetic and gestural repertoire observed in human languages. The Ta-ta theory integrates vocalization and gestural communication elements, offering a more holistic perspective on the multimodal nature of early human communication.

Another influential theory, the Aha! Theory suggests that language originated from a series of "eureka moments" or insights early humans experienced during problem-solving and tool-making activities. According to this hypothesis, linguistic expressions emerged to share and convey these cognitive breakthroughs within the community. The Aha! theory challenges assumptions about the progressive formation of more conventionalized and systematic linguistic structures while agreeing with language use's cognitive and problem-solving components.

While these theories provide diverse perspectives on the origin of language, it is essential to acknowledge the limitations and challenges inherent in unraveling this complex evolutionary puzzle. The scarcity of direct evidence from the distant past and the absence of a clear fossil record for language emergence contribute to the speculative nature of these theories. Furthermore, a thorough explanation incorporating various cognitive, social, and environmental aspects is necessary due to the complex nature of language, which includes phonetics, syntax, semantics, and pragmatics.

Contemporary research draws from a multidisciplinary approach, combining insights from linguistics, anthropology, neuroscience, and cognitive science to gain a more nuanced understanding of the origin of language. Comparative anatomy, the study of hominin fossils, and the cognitive abilities of non-human primates all provide essential information that helps us comprehend how language gradually emerged throughout evolution. New neuroimaging techniques provide insights into the neurological mechanisms underlying language processing, illuminating the complex interactions between brain architecture and language functions.

Language Evolution in Humans

The evolution of language in humans is one of the most profound and intriguing aspects of our cognitive development. While the exact origins of language remain shrouded in the mists of prehistory, a multidisciplinary exploration involving linguistics, anthropology, neuroscience, and archaeology has unearthed valuable insights into the complex journey of language evolution. This section embarks on a voyage through the key milestones and theories that contribute to our understanding of how language, a defining characteristic of Homo sapiens, emerged and evolved over millennia.

One foundational aspect of language evolution revolves around the vocal anatomy of early hominins. The anatomical adaptations that distinguish the vocal tracts of Homo sapiens from those of other primates, such as the descended larynx, are often considered crucial for the production of a wide range of speech sounds. This adaptation helps articulate complex phonetic parts but needs to explain how language came to be. Even if it is a prerequisite, the vocal anatomy is insufficient to explain the complex language abilities possessed by contemporary humans.

The gestural theory posits that language may have evolved through manual gestures rather than vocalizations. Early hominins, lacking the vocal apparatus for sophisticated speech, might have relied on gestures as a primary mode of communication. Observations of contemporary non-human primates—like chimpanzees—who communicate with various gestures lend credence to this notion. In this context, the evolution of language can be seen as a gradual shift from manual gesturing to vocalization, with both modalities eventually intertwining to form a multimodal communication system. The gestural theory underscores the importance of considering multiple modes of communication in the early stages of language evolution.

The emergence of Homo erectus, characterized by a larger brain size and more sophisticated tool-making abilities, is often associated with a potential leap in communicative complexity. Homo erectus may have developed more complex communication networks because of its higher cognitive capacities. Some scholars propose that an early form of protolanguage—a system with rudimentary linguistic elements—may have emerged during this period. This theory, however theoretical, contends that Homo erectus's advances in cognition prepared the way for language's slow progress.

The advent of Homo sapiens, marked by further increases in brain size and cognitive capabilities, is a crucial chapter in the story of language evolution. The cultural evolution hypothesis posits that language, in its complexity and diversity, emerged through a cumulative process of cultural transmission. As early humans engaged in more complex social interactions, a sophisticated communication system became paramount. The slow evolution and improvement of language were probably aided by the transfer of cultural knowledge, which included methods for creating tools, hunting tactics, and social mores.

The cognitive revolution, which occurred approximately 70,000 years ago, represents a significant turning point in the evolution of language. Symbolic behavior, artistic expression, and the creation of complicated tools all increased during this period, pointing to an unparalleled cognitive leap. The emergence of symbolic thinking, reflected in cave art and symbolic artifacts, is often linked to developing a fully-fledged linguistic system. Symbolic representations served as precursors to language, providing a means to express abstract concepts and share complex ideas within the community.

The displacement theory, proposed by linguist Steven Mithen, suggests that early humans possessed domain-specific cognitive modules for various cognitive functions, including social intelligence, tool-making, language, and natural history. This idea states that these cognitive modules functioned separately and without integration. In its early form, language may have been limited to specific domains, such as social communication. The cognitive components progressively came together, creating a cohesive and adaptable language system. The displacement theory offers a cognitive perspective on the modular evolution of language.

The advent of agriculture around 10,000 years ago and the subsequent rise of complex societies brought new challenges and opportunities for linguistic evolution. The increased scale of human communities, the development of written language, and the need for coordination in agriculture and trade all contributed to the expansion and diversification of languages. The co-evolutionary dynamics between linguistic diversity and social complexity underscore the intricate relationship between language and the sociocultural environment.

The discovery of the FOXP2 gene, also known as the "language gene," has given rise to a growing body of research on the genetic perspectives on language evolution. Mutations in the FOXP2 gene have been linked to language impairments in humans. The presence of a similar version of the FOXP2 gene in Neanderthals suggests that this genetic component predates the emergence of Homo sapiens. While the FOXP2 gene is not the sole determinant of language, its role in neural development and language-related functions highlights the interplay between genetic factors and environmental influences in the evolution of language.

According to the social brain concept, the intricacy of human social interactions, particularly within large and interconnected communities, has driven the evolution of advanced cognitive abilities, including language. The need to navigate complex social networks, keep alliances, and discern others' intents may have applied selective pressure to the evolution of an advanced communication system. Language, as a tool for social bonding, coordination, and the exchange of information, became a crucial adaptation in the evolutionary toolkit of Homo sapiens.

Research on brain lateralization has shed light on the neurological underpinnings of language processing in neuroscience. The left hemisphere of the brain, particularly Broca's and Wernicke's areas, is heavily implicated in language production and comprehension. The lateralization of language functions observed in modern humans raises questions about the neurological underpinnings of language in early hominins. However, direct evidence of brain lateralization in extinct human species needs to be included in the archeological record. Therefore, these features of language evolution have to be inferred by scholars.

While the evolutionary pathways of language are multifaceted and intertwined with broader cognitive, social, and environmental contexts, the field continues to grapple with unanswered questions. The absence of a clear fossil record for language, the challenges of inferring cognitive capacities from material artifacts, and the dynamic interplay of genetic and environmental factors contribute to the ongoing complexities of unraveling the story of language evolution.

In conclusion, the evolution of language in humans is a captivating narrative that unfolds across millennia, weaving together anatomical adaptations, cognitive advancements, cultural dynamics, and genetic influences. From the gestural origins of communication to the cognitive revolution, the emergence of symbolic thinking, and the complexities of social interactions, language evolution reflects the ingenuity of the human mind in navigating the challenges and opportunities of our evolutionary journey. The mystery of how Homo sapiens developed this extraordinary ability for communication begs for further investigation and learning as multidisciplinary research illuminates the pathways of language evolution.

Comparative Linguistics and Evolutionary Biology

The intersection of comparative linguistics and evolutionary biology offers a fascinating lens to explore the intertwined evolution of language and life. While linguistics traditionally resides within the realm of humanities and the study of culture, evolutionary biology delves into the biological processes that shape living organisms. The intersection of these fields deepens our comprehension of the fundamental relationships between language and the evolutionary histories of various species. This essay embarks on a journey through the landscapes of comparative linguistics and evolutionary biology, uncovering the shared mechanisms, divergent paths, and symbiotic influences that characterize the evolution of communication in the biological world.

At the heart of comparative linguistics lies the exploration of linguistic diversity across different human languages, seeking to identify commonalities and distinctions that shed light on the universals of language structure and function. This comparative method goes beyond the domain of human languages to include the study of non-human animal communication systems. The intricate mechanisms of genetic variation, natural selection, and adaptation that underpin the biodiversity seen in the living world are negotiated by evolutionary biology, on the other hand. The intersection of these fields invites us to examine the evolutionary strands woven into communication itself.

A cornerstone in the comparative study of languages is the quest to identify linguistic universals—patterns and features that transcend individual languages and cultures. As linguists scrutinize diverse languages' syntax, semantics, and phonetics, they discern recurrent structures and principles that appear to be inherent to human cognition. The universality of specific linguistic features, such as the distinction between nouns and verbs, suggests a shared cognitive foundation that transcends linguistic diversity. This shared cognitive architecture aligns with the principles of evolutionary biology, which posits that commonalities across species often stem from shared ancestry and adaptive solutions to common challenges.

The parallels between linguistic and biological evolution become particularly evident when examining the concept of a language "family." In linguistics, a language family comprises a group of related languages that share a common ancestor. The historical processes of language divergence and the gradual accumulation of linguistic innovations result in the emergence of distinct languages within a family. Similarly, in evolutionary biology, the concept of a biological family encompasses a group of related species descended from a common ancestor. The dynamic processes of diversification and adaptation over time are reflected in the branching patterns seen in both biological and linguistic family trees.

The study of historical linguistics further illuminates the evolutionary nature of language change. Like living things, languages change and evolve throughout successive generations. Sound changes, shifts in grammar, and the emergence of new vocabulary echo the dynamic processes of genetic variation, adaptation, and speciation observed in biological evolution. The principles of descent with modification, a fundamental concept in evolutionary biology, find resonance in the diachronic development of languages, where linguistic forms change over generations.

Evolutionary biologists study the wide range of signaling systems regarding non-human communication that have developed in various species. From the intricate dances of bees to the sonar echolocation of bats, the animal kingdom showcases a rich tapestry of communication strategies shaped by natural selection. Comparative linguistics extends its gaze to non-human communication, seeking to understand animal signals' cognitive and expressive dimensions. The study of animal communication systems reveals convergent evolution, where distantly related species develop similar communication strategies in response to comparable ecological challenges.

One compelling example of convergent evolution in communication is found in the vocal learning abilities of specific bird species and humans. While the vocalizations of birds like songbirds and parrots differ significantly from human speech, the underlying capacity for vocal learning reflects a shared cognitive trait. The neural mechanisms involved in verbal education in birds and humans exhibit striking parallels, suggesting a convergent evolution of this complex cognitive ability. This convergence invites exploration into the genetic and neural foundations of vocal learning and the selective pressures that led to its emergence in different lineages.

The quest for language evolution also studies the FOXP2 gene, often hailed as the "language gene." Mutations in the FOXP2 gene are associated with language impairments in humans, providing a glimpse into the genetic underpinnings of language. Evolutionary biologists study FOXP2's existence and function in non-human animals to learn more about its evolutionary background and possible applications in vocal communication. The intersection of comparative linguistics and evolutionary biology at the genetic level offers insights into the shared genetic toolkit underlying language aspects across different species.

Exploring animal cognition, another frontier in the convergence of linguistics and biology, reveals remarkable cognitive abilities in various species. Dolphins' ability to solve problems, primates' use of tools, and some birds' sophisticated navigational capabilities are examples of multiple creatures' cognitive flexibility and intelligence. By comparing these mental capacities and features of human language usage, comparative linguists contest the conventional wisdom that humans are the only animals with sophisticated cognitive abilities. The discovery of cognitive similarities among different animals highlights how cognitive development has continued throughout existence.

The emergence of syntax, the hierarchical structure of sentences that conveys complex meanings, is a central focus in studying language evolution. The exploration of syntax in human languages, with its recursive and compositional nature, prompts questions about its origins and development. Comparative linguists draw on evidence from the syntax of different languages and the cognitive abilities of non-human animals to trace the evolutionary pathways leading to the emergence of syntactic structures. The investigation into the cognitive prerequisites for syntax and its potential roots in non-human communication systems offers a glimpse into the deep history of this quintessentially human aspect of language.

The convergence of comparative linguistics and evolutionary biology also unfolds in the study of cultural evolution—the transmission of knowledge, behaviors, and innovations within human communities. Cultural shift displays variation, selection, and generational transmission patterns like genetic change. Language development, deeply intertwined with cultural practices and shared knowledge, reflects the dynamic interplay between biological and cultural evolution. The cumulative cultural evolution of language, where innovations build upon existing linguistic structures, mirrors the processes of cultural transmission observed in other aspects of human culture.

To sum up, combining comparative linguistics and evolutionary biology provides insights into the complex interactions between language and the broader domain of life. From identifying linguistic universals to exploring language families, from the genetic foundations of language to the convergent evolution of communication strategies in different species, this interdisciplinary journey unravels the intricate connections between linguistic and biological evolution. As researchers continue to traverse this interdisciplinary terrain, the collaborative exploration of language and life promises not only to deepen our understanding of the evolutionary origins of language but also to illuminate the shared threads that weave through the diverse tapestry of communication across the living world.

Implications for Understanding Modern Languages

The study of linguistic evolution, spanning the historical trajectories of languages from their ancient roots to contemporary expressions, holds profound implications for understanding modern languages. As linguists and scholars delve into the intricate tapestry of language history, they unveil threads of continuity and transformation that connect the past to the present. This section explores the implications of studying linguistic evolution for our comprehension of modern languages, shedding light on how insights from historical linguistics, language change, and the dynamics of language families contribute to a nuanced understanding of the languages we speak today.

One significant implication lies in unraveling the historical layers embedded within modern languages. Like all living things, languages constantly evolve and adapt over time. Studying historical linguistics allows linguists to trace the evolutionary paths of languages, uncovering linguistic fossils and reconstructing ancestral forms. By examining the historical development of vocabulary, grammar, and phonetics, linguists can discern the influences of contact with other languages, cultural shifts, and socio-political changes on the linguistic landscape. This historical perspective provides a window into the forces that have shaped and molded the languages we use in the contemporary world.

Language change, a natural and ongoing phenomenon, represents another dimension of linguistic evolution with direct implications for understanding modern languages. The mechanisms of language change, such as sound shifts, semantic drift, and grammatical transformations, unfold over generations, leading to variations in linguistic structures. The study of language change allows linguists to identify patterns of innovation and diffusion, revealing how linguistic features spread through communities and across regions. Linguists can identify the elements that propel linguistic innovation and the persistence of particular linguistic forms throughout time by analyzing the trajectories of language change.

A fundamental idea in historical linguistics is that language families provide essential insights into the relationships between present languages and their ancestral origins. Languages with a common ancestry form a language family, reflecting a historical divergence from a common source. The comparative method, a tool employed in historical linguistics, enables the reconstruction of protolanguages—the hypothetical ancestral languages from which modern languages within a family descend. The study of language families illuminates the shared linguistic heritage of diverse languages and provides a framework for understanding their relationships. For example, the Indo-European language family encompasses languages as varied as English, Hindi, Russian, and Spanish, tracing their origins to a common ancestor spoken thousands of years ago.

Understanding linguistic evolution also enhances our grasp of language contact and the dynamics of linguistic borrowing. Languages are in constant interaction, and the historical record reveals instances of contact between different linguistic communities. Language convergence, code-switching, and loanword studies provide insight into how languages impact one another. Languages spoken now frequently bear the marks of past interactions, whether through migration, trade, or cultural interchange. By untangling the webs of language contact, linguists gain insights into the cross-cultural fertilization of languages and how linguistic diversity is preserved and enriched.

Studying linguistic evolution contributes to understanding linguistic typology—the classification of languages based on their structural features. By examining the diversity of linguistic structures across different language families and regions, linguists identify common patterns and variations. Through a comparative method that goes beyond linguistic boundaries, researchers can identify universal principles of language organization and learn how languages change to fulfill communication needs. Linguistic typology provides a framework for understanding the range of structural possibilities within human languages and highlights how languages exhibit both similarities and distinctiveness.

Moreover, insights from linguistic evolution offer valuable perspectives on the factors influencing language stability and change. Some languages undergo relatively slow and gradual changes, while others experience more rapid transformations. The sociolinguistic context, language vitality, and level of language contact significantly shape the trajectory of linguistic evolution. By examining the historical forces that have contributed to the persistence or transformation of languages, scholars acquire a greater comprehension of the resilience and adaptability of linguistic systems. This knowledge is particularly relevant in language revitalization efforts, where an awareness of historical patterns can inform strategies for preserving endangered languages.

The study of linguistic evolution also intersects with the burgeoning field of computational linguistics and natural language processing. For training machine learning models that aim to comprehend and produce language similar to humans, historical linguistics offers valuable data. The principles of linguistic evolution, such as regular sound changes and morphological transformations, inform algorithms designed to analyze linguistic data and detect patterns of language change. As technology advances, the synergy between historical linguistics and computational methods holds promise for enhancing our ability to explore linguistic evolution on a larger scale and across diverse language families.

Furthermore, the insights gained from studying linguistic evolution contribute to a more nuanced understanding of linguistic diversity and language endangerment. As languages evolve, some face the risk of extinction due to various factors, including cultural assimilation, language shift, and globalization. The historical perspectives provided by linguistic evolution enable scholars to trace the trajectories of endangered languages, understand the forces that have contributed to their decline, and explore strategies for language revitalization. By connecting the present challenges of linguistic diversity to their historical roots, researchers can develop more informed and effective interventions to support endangered languages.

In summary, there are ramifications for linguistic evolution research that go across many aspects of our comprehension of contemporary languages. From uncovering historical layers and patterns of language change to illuminating the relationships between language families and the dynamics of language contact, the exploration of linguistic evolution enriches our comprehension of the languages we use today. As scholars continue to navigate the intricate landscapes of linguistic history, they unveil the threads that connect the past to the present, offering a profound tapestry of insights into the enduring evolution of human language.

Chapter VIII

Future Trends in Linguistics

Advances in Computational Linguistics

The field of computational linguistics, at the intersection of linguistics and computer science, has undergone remarkable advances, transforming how we interact with language and harnessing the power of technology to unravel linguistic complexities. This section explores the critical developments in computational linguistics, from foundational concepts to cutting-edge applications, shedding light on how these advances shape our understanding of language, enable natural language processing, and open new frontiers in human-computer interaction.

At its core, computational linguistics seeks to close the gap between machine and human comprehension. The journey begins with the foundational concept of natural language processing (NLP), which involves equipping computers with the ability to comprehend, interpret, and generate human language. Early developments in computational linguistics focused on rule-based approaches, where linguistic rules and grammatical structures were manually encoded to guide machines in language analysis. While effective to some extent, these rule-based systems faced limitations in handling natural language nuances, ambiguities, and dynamic nature.

The advent of statistical methods marked a paradigm shift in computational linguistics. Machine learning techniques, particularly probabilistic models, gained prominence, allowing computers to learn patterns and associations from vast amounts of linguistic data. Corpus linguistics, the study of large bodies of text, became a cornerstone for training models in statistical NLP. This shift towards data-driven approaches paved the way for developing more robust and flexible systems capable of handling diverse linguistic phenomena.

One of the breakthroughs in computational linguistics is the rise of machine translation. Machine translation systems struggled with linguistic nuances and idiomatic expressions, often producing translations that needed more fluency and accuracy. The introduction of statistical machine translation (SMT) and, later, neural machine translation (NMT) revolutionized the landscape. These approaches leverage large parallel corpora to learn translation patterns, enabling systems to generate more contextually accurate and linguistically natural translations. Neural networks' ability to capture complex relationships within data has propelled machine translation to unprecedented performance levels.

The introduction of deep learning, A subfield of machine learning that draws inspiration from the composition and operation of the human brain, has been a transformative force in computational linguistics. Deep neural networks, particularly recurrent neural networks (RNNs) and transformers, have demonstrated exceptional capabilities in capturing sequential and long-range dependencies in language. These architectures excel in language modeling, sentiment analysis, and named entity recognition tasks. Since its introduction in models such as BERT (Bidirectional Encoder Representations from Transformers), the transformer architecture has established new standards for comprehending contextual data and linguistic subtleties.

The integration of linguistics and deep learning is evident in developing pre-trained language models. Models like GPT (Generative Pre-trained Transformer) and T5 (Text-to-Text Transfer Transformer) are pre-trained on vast amounts of text data, learning contextualized representations of words and phrases. These models exhibit remarkable performance in various language tasks and can be fine-tuned for specific applications, from question answering to text summarization. The era of pre-trained language models signifies a shift towards more generalized and adaptable language understanding.

Computational linguistics has also made significant strides in sentiment analysis and emotion detection. Sentiment analysis algorithms, powered by machine learning, can decipher the emotional tone of text, whether in social media posts, customer reviews, or news articles. These tools enable businesses to gauge public opinion, marketers to understand customer sentiment, and researchers to analyze emotional trends in textual data. The ability to discern emotion enhances our understanding of user-generated content and has implications for brand management, public relations, and social science research.

Another frontier in computational linguistics is the exploration of linguistic creativity through generative models. Creating original, contextually relevant material is critical to creative language generation. GPT-3, one of the most significant language models, has demonstrated astonishing creative writing, poetry generation, and code generation capabilities. These models' capacity to produce logical and contextually relevant text showcases their potential in diverse, innovative applications, from content creation to personalized conversational agents.

The application of computational linguistics extends beyond traditional language domains into the analysis of multimodal data. Multimodal models have gained popularity because they incorporate data from visuals, audio, and text in addition to other modalities. These models enable a more comprehensive understanding and interpretation of content in various contexts, from image captioning to video analysis. The combination of language and multimodal data promises to enhance our experiences with the digital world as technology develops.

Moreover, advances in computational linguistics have paved the way for innovations in human-computer interaction. Conversational agents, or chatbots powered by natural language understanding and generation models, have become integral parts of customer service, virtual assistants, and interactive applications. The ability to converse fluently and contextually with users represents a significant leap in the quest for human-like interactions between machines and humans. These apps not only improve user experiences but also pave the way for technologies that are more accessible and inclusive.

Ethical considerations have emerged as a crucial dimension in computational linguistics. Bias in language models, whether in terms of gender, race, or cultural nuances, poses challenges that demand careful attention. Researchers and practitioners in computational linguistics are actively engaged in addressing bias, promoting fairness, and enhancing transparency in language technologies. Ethical frameworks and norms are being developed to guarantee that the advantages of computational linguistics are shared fairly and that technology is in line with society's values.

In conclusion, the advances in computational linguistics represent a journey from rule-based systems to data-driven models, from statistical approaches to the transformative power of deep learning. The synergy between linguistics and technology has propelled us into an era where machines can understand and generate human-like language. From machine translation and sentiment analysis to creative language generation and multimodal understanding, computational linguistics continues to redefine our relationship with language and technology. As the field evolves, the ethical considerations surrounding language technologies become increasingly vital, emphasizing the need for responsible development and deployment. In its exploration of the boundaries between language and technology, computing linguistics is a monument to the unique opportunities that arise from the union of linguistic knowledge with computing power.

Neurolinguistics and Brain-Computer Interfaces

A novel frontier in investigating and manipulating the complex link between language and the human brain is the nexus of neurolinguistics and brain-computer interfaces (BCIs). Neurolinguistics, the study of the neural mechanisms underlying language processing, delves into the neural substrates of language comprehension, production, and representation. However, direct brain-to-external device connection is now possible because of advancements in brain-computer interface technology. This essay explores the synergy between neurolinguistics and brain-computer interfaces, unraveling the potential implications for enhancing communication, decoding language from neural signals, and restoring language function in individuals with neurological disorders.

The goal of understanding the brain architecture underlying language is at the heart of neurolinguistics. Techniques for functional neuroimaging, like functional magnetic resonance imaging (fMRI) and magnetoencephalography (MEG), have enabled researchers to pinpoint brain regions associated with language processing. The traditional theory of language localization, which suggested separate brain regions for various language activities, has given way to a more dispersed and networked understanding. Neuroimaging studies reveal the dynamic and collaborative engagement of multiple brain regions in language tasks, emphasizing the complexity of the neural network that underlies our linguistic abilities.

Technological developments in neuroimaging have made it easier to study brain activity in real-time while performing linguistic tasks.

Electroencephalography (EEG) and event-related potentials (ERPs) offer high temporal resolution, allowing researchers to examine the millisecond-by-millisecond dynamics of language processing. These methods explain the phases of language processing, from early perceptual analysis to more advanced syntactic and semantic integration. The marriage of neurolinguistics and neuroimaging has thus ushered in an era where the intricacies of language processing can be observed with unprecedented detail.

The synergy between neurolinguistics and brain-computer interfaces comes to the forefront with the emergence of BCIs designed to decode language from neural signals. For those suffering from illnesses like severe paralysis or amyotrophic lateral sclerosis (ALS), which impair conventional modes of communication, invasive brain-computer interfaces (BCIs) show potential. These BCIs can translate the user's thoughts into text or speech by capturing neural activity associated with language production or intention. This transformative technology can potentially restore communication and autonomy to individuals who have lost the ability to speak or move.

Non-invasive BCIs, which capture neural signals from the scalp, have also ventured into language decoding. fNIRS (functional near-infrared spectroscopy) and electroencephalography (EEG) are two non-invasive methods investigated to see if language-related information can be extracted from brain activity. Although non-invasive brain-computer interfaces (BCIs) might not attain the same degree of accuracy as their invasive counterparts, their accessibility and safety make them feasible choices for a broader range of individuals. The prospect of typing or communicating through imagined speech using non-invasive BCIs opens doors for individuals with motor disabilities, offering an alternative means of expression.

The symbiosis of neurolinguistics and BCIs extends beyond communication restoration to the realm of augmentative and alternative communication (AAC). Individuals with locked-in syndrome, where voluntary muscle control is severely impaired, may benefit from BCIs that enable them to select letters, words, or commands directly from their neural activity. By combining language models and predictive algorithms with BCIs, users may communicate more effectively and express themselves more precisely. This intersection of language neuroscience and assistive technology exemplifies the potential for BCIs to augment and amplify our communicative capacities.

Moreover, exploring neural interfaces for language processing has implications for decoding internal speech and language representation. Brain-computer interfaces have been employed to reconstruct perceived or imagined speech from neural signals. Researchers aim to unravel the neural code that represents linguistic content in the mind by decoding the neural patterns associated with specific phonemes or words. This endeavor advances our understanding of how the brain encodes language and opens avenues for developing BCIs that can translate internal thoughts into external language without the need for overt speech.

In the context of neurorehabilitation, the synergy between neurolinguistics and BCIs holds promise for individuals recovering from stroke or other neurological injuries affecting language function. Protocols for language therapy can benefit from integrating BCIs to offer individualized and focused interventions. For example, BCIs that provide real-time feedback on brain activity associated with language tasks can enhance neuroplasticity and support the reorganization of neural circuits involved in language processing. This method maximizes the effectiveness of language rehabilitation by utilizing the concepts of neurofeedback.

When developing and implementing BCIs for language decoding, ethical issues come up. Concerns about permission, privacy, and possible abuse of neurological data highlight the significance of moral standards and legal frameworks. Ensuring the security and confidentiality of neural information is paramount, especially as BCIs become more prevalent in various aspects of healthcare and daily life. Striking a balance between the transformative potential of BCIs and safeguarding individuals' autonomy and privacy is a critical facet of responsible development in this field.

The Role of AI in Language Processing

The confluence of language and artificial intelligence (AI) processing is a testament to technology's transformative power in unraveling human communication's complexities. AI, driven by machine learning algorithms and natural language processing (NLP) techniques, has emerged as a formidable force in understanding, interpreting, and generating human language. The numerous ways that artificial intelligence (AI) is used in language processing are examined in this section, along with the development of language technologies, their prospects and problems, and their significant influence on several facets of our daily lives.

At the heart of AI's role in language processing lies the evolution of machine learning models that underpin natural language understanding. Early AI systems relied on rule-based approaches, where explicit linguistic rules were programmed to govern language analysis. While effective in specific contexts, these rule-based systems needed help to cope with natural language nuances, ambiguities, and intricacies. The advent of statistical approaches, particularly machine learning, marked a paradigm shift.

Large volumes of linguistic data have been utilized to teach algorithms for machine learning, allowing them to recognize the structures, relationships, and patterns unique to language. Supervised learning, where models are trained on labeled datasets, will enable algorithms to discern relationships between input data and desired outputs. Conversely, unsupervised learning enables models to recognize structures and patterns in data without explicit instruction. The marriage of machine learning and linguistic data paved the way for advancements in language understanding, enabling AI systems to comprehend and generate human-like text with increasing accuracy.

Natural language processing, a subfield of AI, focuses on equipping machines with the ability to interact with human language. The progression from rule-based parsing to statistical models and, more recently, to deep learning architectures has revolutionized the landscape of NLP. Recurrent neural networks (RNNs) and transformer architectures, such as BERT (Bidirectional Encoder Representations from Transformers), have demonstrated exceptional capabilities in capturing contextual information, syntactic structures, and semantic nuances in language. These models excel in tasks ranging from language translation and sentiment analysis to question answering and summarization.

One of the prominent applications of AI in language processing is machine translation. The goal of removing language barriers and promoting intercultural communication has propelled the development of machine translation technology. Statistical machine translation (SMT) paved the way, and the advent of neural machine translation (NMT) further elevated translation accuracy and fluency. AI-driven translation systems, such as Google Translate, have become integral tools for global communication, enabling users to translate text between multiple languages with remarkable fidelity.

Sentiment analysis, another facet of AI in language processing, involves discerning textual content's emotional tone or sentiment. Whether analyzing customer reviews, social media posts, or news articles, sentiment analysis algorithms can categorize text as positive, negative, or neutral. This technology is leveraged in diverse domains, from business and marketing to public opinion research, providing insights into the emotional context surrounding textual data.

Chatbots and virtual assistants driven by artificial intelligence are one example of how language processing technologies are used in human-computer interaction. These conversational bots can read user questions, deliver information, and carry out activities thanks to their natural language comprehension. Artificial intelligence (AI)--powered chatbots are being integrated into e-commerce sites, customer support departments, and other applications to provide quick and responsive consumer care.

The evolution of AI in language processing also extends to the realm of creative content generation. Generative models, such as OpenAI's GPT (Generative Pre-trained Transformer) series, have demonstrated the ability to produce coherent and contextually relevant text. These models can be optimized for creative tasks, such as composing stories and poems or creating code because they have already been pre-trained on large datasets. The implications for content creation, personalized recommendations, and even human-like conversational agents are profound.

Despite the remarkable progress, AI in language processing faces challenges, chief among them being the issue of bias. Language models trained on large and diverse datasets may inadvertently learn and perpetuate biases in the data. Gender, racial, or cultural preferences may manifest in the generated text, raising ethical concerns and necessitating scrutiny and mitigation strategies. Researchers and developers are actively engaged in addressing bias to ensure fairness and inclusivity in language technologies.

Another difficulty for AI in language processing is multilingualism. While major languages often receive extensive attention in model training, languages with smaller speaker populations or unique linguistic characteristics may be underrepresented. Efforts to develop language technologies encompassing a broader range of languages and dialects are crucial for ensuring equitable access and functionality across linguistic diversity.

The direction artificial intelligence is taking in language processing has the potential to improve human-technology interactions. The integration of AI-driven language models into educational tools, content recommendation systems, and healthcare applications represents avenues for positive impact. AI technologies can assist language learners, offer personalized content suggestions, and aid in medical diagnosis through the analysis of textual data.

Emerging Fields and Interdisciplinary Approaches

The landscape of academic inquiry is undergoing a profound transformation, marked by the emergence of new fields and a growing emphasis on interdisciplinary approaches. This section investigates the dynamics of these new areas, the forces that gave rise to them, and how multidisciplinary cooperation has revolutionized the search for knowledge. Scholars are becoming more interested in intersections—where different viewpoints come together to confront complex problems and reveal previously undiscovered aspects of the world—as traditional discipline boundaries become less clear.

A prominent development in higher education is the emergence of disciplines beyond conventional disciplinary boundaries. Interdisciplinary studies, such as environmental science, bioinformatics, and cognitive neuroscience, have gained prominence as scholars recognize the limitations of siloed approaches in addressing complex, real-world problems. These topics function at the intersection of several academic disciplines, combining knowledge from several fields to provide thorough and integrated viewpoints. For instance, environmental science integrates sociology, physics, chemistry, and biology to comprehend the complex interactions between human cultures and the environment. By recognizing the interdependence of systems, this holistic approach promotes a more sophisticated comprehension of complicated events.

The motivation behind the emergence of these interdisciplinary fields is rooted in the recognition that many contemporary challenges are inherently multifaceted. Issues such as climate change, public health crises, and technological advancements often require a synthesis of knowledge from various disciplines to be effectively understood and addressed. Interdisciplinary approaches enable researchers to navigate the complexity of these challenges, leveraging a spectrum of methodologies and frameworks to develop comprehensive solutions. This departure from traditional disciplinary boundaries represents a paradigm shift, emphasizing collaboration and integration as essential to scholarly inquiry.

The convergence of the humanities with STEM (science, technology, engineering, and mathematics) sectors demonstrates the interdisciplinary character of new fields. The intersection of these traditionally distinct domains has given rise to digital humanities, where scholars apply computational methods to analyze and interpret cultural artifacts, literature, and historical data. Integrating quantitative and qualitative methods deepens our comprehension of human history and culture while demonstrating the transformative power of interdisciplinary cooperation to increase the breadth of scholarly research.

Moreover, the fusion of disciplines extends beyond the sciences and humanities to embrace social sciences and the arts. For instance, the field of neuroaesthetics explores the neural mechanisms underlying aesthetic experiences, bridging neuroscience and art appreciation. Neuroaesthetics exemplifies how interdisciplinary approaches can shed light on the intricate relationships between seemingly disparate realms of human experience by examining the interplay between cognitive processes and artistic expressions. The synergies between disciplines create a fertile ground for innovation and uncovering novel insights that might remain elusive within the confines of individual fields.

Technology has been a significant factor in making transdisciplinary research easier. Computational tools, data analytics, and simulation techniques provide researchers with powerful means to integrate diverse datasets, model complex systems, and analyze phenomena across multiple scales. The interdisciplinary marriage of technology and traditional disciplines has given rise to fields like computational social science, where large-scale data analysis and computer modeling are employed to study human behavior and societal dynamics. These cutting-edge approaches open up new lines of inquiry by enabling academics to investigate issues beyond the confines of their particular fields of study.

Interdisciplinary research is not solely confined to the sciences but has also permeated business, policy, and ethics. For example, the field of business ethics draws on insights from philosophy, economics, and organizational studies to navigate the ethical challenges corporations face. Interdisciplinary approaches to business ethics promote a more nuanced understanding of the many ethical issues within the corporate environment by combining a variety of viewpoints. In a highly linked and quickly changing global economic environment, the importance of this interdisciplinary lens for guiding moral decision-making is becoming more widely acknowledged.

Despite the transformative potential of interdisciplinary research, it comes with its challenges. Traditionally, academic institutions have been organized according to their respective disciplines' departments, funding sources, and publishing houses. Funding for studies that cross traditional disciplinary boundaries is one of the institutional obstacles that interdisciplinary scholars frequently encounter. Additionally, the assessment and recognition of multidisciplinary work within traditional academic metrics can be complex, posing challenges for researchers seeking educational advancement. Efforts to bridge these institutional gaps, such as establishing interdisciplinary research centers and collaborative funding initiatives, are essential for creating an encouraging atmosphere for multidisciplinary scholars.

Additionally, conducting interdisciplinary research necessitates being open to navigating different disciplinary epistemologies, techniques, and languages. As academics from many backgrounds try to find common ground and shared understandings, effective communication becomes increasingly important. Building a common language and respecting each discipline's distinctive contributions are essential to the collaborative process. Interdisciplinary teams that successfully navigate these challenges often produce more robust, innovative research capable of addressing the multifaceted nature of complex problems.

Beyond the classroom, multidisciplinary techniques can change society's problems. Grand societal challenges, such as climate change, healthcare disparities, and global pandemics, are inherently complex and interconnected. Addressing these challenges requires collaboration across disciplines, bringing together experts from diverse fields to develop comprehensive solutions. Multidisciplinary study is a scholarly pursuit and a social necessity, as it acknowledges that the answers to several modern issues are found at the nexus of various knowledge disciplines.

Conclusion

In conclusion, "Unlocking Language: From Syntax to Semantics - A Comprehensive Exploration" has sought to unravel the intricate tapestry of human communication, delving into the fundamental building blocks of language—syntax and semantics. Throughout this comprehensive journey, we've navigated the rich historical roots of speech, the intricate dance between syntax and semantics, and the profound influence of language on our cognitive processes, cultural expressions, and technological advancements.

The exploration of syntax has allowed us to appreciate the intricate structures that underpin every sentence we construct, showcasing the universality and cultural diversity encapsulated within grammatical frameworks. From the simplicity of subject-verb-object constructions to the complexity of syntactic variations across languages, we've discovered how syntax is the scaffolding for effective communication.

Simultaneously, the investigation into semantics has unraveled the nuanced world of meaning-making. We've seen how words, with their complex meanings, influence our attitudes, interactions, and perceptions. The exploration of semantic fields has illustrated the contextual fluidity of language, shedding light on the dynamic nature of communication that extends beyond mere words to encompass cultural nuances and societal intricacies.

As we consider the interplay between syntax and semantics, a profound understanding emerges—an experience that language is more than just a means of communication and a dynamic force that shapes our thoughts, influences our relationships, and drives societal progress. The voyage has spanned fields beyond linguistics, including neurology, AI, and cross-cultural communication, illustrating the ubiquitous influence of language on many aspects of our lives.

As readers close the chapters of "Unlocking Language," I hope this exploration catalyses continued curiosity and engagement with the boundless realm of language. Whether enhancing practical language skills, navigating the evolving landscape of communication technologies, or fostering cross-cultural understanding, unlocking language is an ongoing and enriching endeavor. In this dynamic landscape, the key to effective communication lies in understanding the rules of syntax and semantics and embracing the ever-evolving, vibrant tapestry of human expression.

Thank you for buying and reading/listening to our book.
If you found this book useful/helpful please take a few minutes
and leave a review on the platform where you purchased our book.
Your feedback matters greatly to us.

www.ingramcontent.com/pod-product-compliance
Lightning Source LLC
Chambersburg PA
CBHW071509150726
48000CB00002B/508